More Vegetarian Dinner Parties

Leon Lewis

Free Range Publishing

D1351028

First published 1998

To contact the author about the book, availability of wines or
personal appearances, please write to him:
Leon Lewis, 132b London Road, Brentwood, Essex CM14 4NS
or telephone **01277 218661**

Free Range Publishing
66 High Street, Great Baddow, Chelmsford, Essex CM2 7HH
Tel: 01245 478660
email: dave.designs @dial.pipex.com

British Library Cataloguing in Publication Data
A catalogue record for this book is available from the British Library

ISBN 1-872979 01 7

Printed and bound in Eire
by
Colour Books Limited

Contents

Chapter 4

**A Festive Feast
(Cold Menu)**

Chapter 5

A Dinner for Phil

Chapter 6

A 'Sticky' Dinner

Chapter 7

A Mediterranean Dinner Party

Chapter 8

A Finger-Food Party

Chapter 9

A Vegetarian Barbecue/Picnic

Chapter 12

Guest Recipes

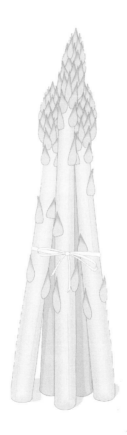

"Vegetables are <u>not</u> boring!"

Introduction

I begin this introduction with an apology to all those hundreds of people who have asked me in the past few years "When are you going to write another book?" It has been a long while since *Vegetarian Dinner Parties* was first on sale in June 1983. I would like to thank Thorsons for having faith in me then, after I was a little depressed in my search for a publisher. Indeed, one was "kind" enough to send me a critique of my script amongst which were the words "How treacherous a misconception could be the whole concept of a vegetarian dinner party. Do vegetarians congregate thus out of self defence or for whatever other reason in sufficient numbers to justify a special publication?" After the "black" edition sold well, they decided to up-date the book in 1987. It may sound strange, but I am most grateful to them for allowing me to take over the publication of the book myself when they were taken over by Collins in 1989. I was, indeed, fortunate to have the help and support of such a talented friend, Dave Whitby, who skilfully used transparencies that I had commissioned in the late 70's while trying out my dinner party ideas at the Windsor Lodge Hotel in Swansea. These were incorporated into a further up-date of the text with a handful of new ideas, but changes to the original format were minimal. I have signed and sold many thousand copies of these and because I felt so comfortable with its contents and enjoyed cooking all the dishes from it, I felt no need to expand into new areas.

> " How treacherous a misconception could be the whole concept of a vegetarian dinner party. Do vegetarians congregate thus out of self defence – or for whatever other reason in sufficient numbers – to justify a special publication? "

Apart from the impatient requests from fans who are now looking to me for new ideas, it is the amount of travel that I have done in the 90's that has been the major spur to translating my discoveries of the last few years onto paper. As will become apparent from the introductions to the various chapters, new friends and old in France have been a major source of ideas but it is the continuing friendship, support and inspiration of my dear friend Bernard (now a resident of Sydney), who helped so much with my first book, that has pushed me into this new venture which has been completed within 83 days of my return from my latest holiday 'down under'. A tribute should also go to Dave who has also been badgering me for a while to sit down and write. His competence and flair has given me the confidence to concentrate

"Vegetarian food is not boring!"

wholeheartedly on the menu planning, recipes and research while he puts his talents to the job of presenting the script in the most practical way.

There are countless other friends and people I have met fleetingly at festivals, demonstrations and other events who have helped me with ideas and constructive criticism. However dismissive I may be at the time that the advice is delivered, I want to put on record that every idea is taken on board and sometimes acted on immediately, sometimes put on the back burner to surface some time later. I have never deviated from my cause to bring vegetarian gourmet food to as many people as possible and I am forever grateful to all the average fifteen thousand people who eat my food each year. Whether it is when feeding around 200 people an hour (as happened at the WOMAD Festival in Reading in July 1997) or when cooking for a more intimate event such as a 21st Birthday Dinner Party for just six people when I was invited also to choose wines to accompany the meal, I take great joy from the positive feedback from those that have enjoyed my food. This book will, I hope, greatly increase the number of people who will indulge themselves and prove that vegetarian food is not boring.

Just as with *Vegetarian Dinner Parties* and in all my catering work, I have used wholefoods in my recipes in this book wherever possible. I believe that to be a good cook you need the finest ingredients and a vegetarian gourmet's store cupboard should contain a huge range of spices, herbs, oils, vinegars, grains, pulses, nuts and dried fruit.

Many of these items keep for months in a cool place and a simple dish can be transformed with a few judicious additions. For instance, a green salad is elevated by the addition of a few pumpkin seeds and soaked and slivered sun-dried tomatoes.

> **" Very few of the dishes in this book will be outside the capabilities of anyone for reasons of non-availability of the ingredients "**

I also go along with my friend Andreas Michli's philosophy that everything you eat should be for a reason. This is an anti-junkfood philosophy which many people today would not understand. Perhaps, most of all, a vegetarian gourmet cook needs a reliable source of fresh vegetables and fruit, and here I am very lucky to have the finest and freshest produce from Nick Hammond who delivers to my door whenever I make an order and Mike Gibber who runs a vibrant and interesting business in Holloway, London. On my travels, too, I am lucky to have an excellent supplier in Banbury for the Fairport Festival (i.e. Terry Griffin) and I have found other top quality traders around the country. For a range of produce and for freshness, the local supermarkets here in the U.K. (and in the other countries that I have travelled) do a marvellous job. Very few of the dishes in this book will be outside the capabilities of anyone for reasons of non-availability of the ingredients.

As will become apparent whilst you wade through the introductions and recipes in this book, I have developed a great interest in the collection and use of wild ingredients. The many woods, parks and country lanes around my home in Brentwood abound with much that can be used in the kitchen. Most of all, it is the wonder of mushrooms that occupies much of my time in the wetter months of the year. It is a highly transportable interest and I have enjoyed many a walk in foreign countryside more because of the possibility of discoverying something that might be good to eat. It is also an interest that I am keen to pass on and I regularly invite people to join me for a foray and some time afterwards in my kitchen enjoying wine and the fruits of our walk. It is a most social few hours.

A most pleasant dinner party gathering at Branxton in the Hunter Valley NSW with Bernard, Roger (Cellar Door Manager, Brokenwood Wines), Sue (C.D.M. Allandale), Helen (Chateau Pato) and Nick.

The other great interest that I have developed since *Vegetarian Dinner Parties* was first published is wine. I may have had an interest before, but to this has been added the knowledge that comes through having several good teachers. Many of them will be mentioned later on and there will be many references to those wines that I have loved and drunk. Here I will pay homage to those with whom I have dined in Branxton, near Cessnock in the Hunter Valley in Australia, the home of Roger and Sue. I recall many an excellent tasting at the Rothbury Winery and these occasions were made memorable as much by the friendly ways of the cellar door staff as by the fine wines that we tasted. John Sykes soon took Bernard and myself under his wing and showed us some of the great aging qualities of the Chardonnays and Pinot Noirs of the Hunter. Very generously, he offered to ship a dozen bottles back to the U.K., free of charge, to help me learn more about this. Fifteen year old Semillons were much appreciated along with some even older reds. Roger Paterson, also then at Rothbury, invited me to visit him for a meal in January 1995. The meal was made in Sydney and transported by bus up to Cessnock. A short journey to Branxton in Roger's Volvo and a short time in Sue and Roger's kitchen was the prelude to a sumptious evening. Sue re-introduced me to the delights of Allandale where she is cellar door manager. John and his wife, Beth, were part of the entertainment and Roger's brother, Nick, represented the wonderful Brokenwood winery where he works. Dishes which you will find in this book were driven forward with superb wines such as a 1974 Lakes Folly Red and a 1984 Allandale Semillon. That evening I was introduced to the game "Options" where a wine is served "blind" either having been decanted or with foil around to obscure its label and shape of bottle. The perpetrator then asks questions about the wine of the type "Is it Australian, French or Californian?" The whole evening and two subsequent ones there have been great fun and thanks to all involved for some happy memories. I am lucky enough to be able to further my interest in Australian wine in the U.K. through the efforts of the Australian Wine Company. They are helpful at all times and have an excellent list. Moreover, they run the Great Australian Wine Tasting each May at which many different wines may be sampled and many winemakers are there in person.

> **"I have seen many changes over the eighteen years involved with these outdoor events"**

Because of my overseas trips, my year has a lovely roundness about it. The summer is occupied with festivals and all that they entail. Because all the food served on my stall is produced by me, it takes a month and five freezers to prepare for some of the larger events. I have seen many changes over the eighteen years involved with these outdoor events, not all of them good. The notes that I have made in Chapter Ten express my thoughts in this direction. In between the summer months and my January holiday to the antipodes, I have for some fourteen years undertaken a tour of hotels, colleges, village halls, schools and clubs demonstrating the tricks of my trade to anyone who wants to listen. These have evolved little over time except that distances now seem much less than in the early years when I thought nothing of a trip to

Leon in action at a cookery demonstration

Scotland, Yorkshire or Swansea. Now, of course, I shall have a whole new book to demonstrate. The average attendances at these evenings (for they nearly all are evening events) is 80 and, at the rate of around 50 a year, that is 4000 people who sit patiently listening to my philosophy, advice and jokes waiting for the serving of the food. I was lucky enough to have collected many a schoolboy howler in a previous life and they are the best warm up lines that I know. Lines like – *"Socrates died from an overdose of wedlock"* and *"Name a vehicle for carrying the sick?   A bucket"* – are priceless, and I thank all those who contributed to this great collection.

A demonstration reaches its conclusion and the audience is still awake!

When I am planning a dinner party, I work out the menu, shopping list and then prepare space in the kitchen. Generally, I work on desserts first and leave baking to last so that the oven is used once only. Also I work early on any dishes that might benefit from time. Some planning may help you make best use of time and time is a commodity which needs more "weighing" than the ingredients themselves. When guests arrive, I like to have some food to hand round, entrées, to accompany the first drink and it does make sense to give the guests some idea of the extent of the meal so that they can "pace" themselves from the first course. A first course that can be plated up and placed on the table has several advantages. A white and a large red wine glass should be provided and a jug of water (or more if you have a large number of guests). Separate glasses for water should not be necessary as the red wine glass may be used at the start of the meal and the white wine glass later. If guests bring a red that is too cool to drink, try immersing it in a bowl of warm water. A warm white can be chilled quickly on some ice but fine Chardonnays are often served too cold; 13°C is a good temperature. It is an excellent idea to appoint someone to open the wine and top up as necessary while you worry about the food. The same plate is used throughout in France where bread has the function of cleaning up the plates. This is most practical. I have as much preparation for coffee and meal endings done before guests arrive and I have clear surfaces ready for dirty plates. This is where a dishwasher can be used to help clear things as you go along. And I do everything that I can to ensure that I enjoy myself throughout the meal.

The hardest aspect of writing up my recipes is giving weights and volumes. Not only is it not my style to weigh or measure, it actually doubles the time to create a dinner party. I have done my best to check all of the measurements given herein but I apologise, in advance, for any errors in this area. Where weights are given for prepared ingredients e.g. the cooked Sushi rice in Chapter Five, then it is to the **prepared** weight that I refer. Note that I have not indicated quantities of salt as it is very much a matter of personal taste how much salt is needed for a recipe and I like to discourage the over-use of salt. All recipes are intended for six people, but, just as I advised in the Introduction to *Vegetarian Dinner Parties*, it all rather depends on whether you do a chapter in its entirety as to whether you will have much food left over, and much of the food freezes well.

Finally, I have to pay my respects to the many labour saving devices that make my work possible. I use a range of food processors from a huge and heavy Crypto Peerless which will make over a kilogram of pastry at a time to a standard Magimix and a special machine which cooks as well as processing. A further Crypto machine does heavy slicing and shredding and, although not suitable for home use, it is invaluable at the festivals, turning a 12.5 kilogram sack of carrots into small dice in a matter of minutes. Two Brother combination microwave ovens do much of the light cooking work. Five freezers of different vintages are filled up during the early summer ready for the busy times ahead and last, but not least, my cleaners, Jean and Jim, willingly take on all cleaning jobs, even pots that have cooked a weekend of curries.

*A typical Lebanese spread – Greek Flat Bread, Hummus, Mutabbal,
Spinach Triangles, Stuffed Vine Leaves and Falafels.*

Chapter One

The Lebanese Feast

The inspiration for this feast came from many visits to some wonderful Lebanese restaurants in London and the helpfulness of staff at the restaurants in advising on ingredients, method and presentation. The meal has no centre piece. Rather more, it is a collection of dishes which are packed with colour, flavour, texture and the healthiest of ingredients dominated by olive oil, lemon juice and garlic. At the Phoenicia in Kensington, you are presented immediately with a bowl of very fresh cos lettuce, baby (Lebanese) cucumbers, radishes, chillis and beef tomatoes and a selection of olives and other pickles while you choose your meze items. I do not ever recall reading the menu at the Phoenicia (but my friends will comment that I rarely read a menu anywhere) for you are quite safe to rely on the manager, Hani, to select a balanced meze which is suitable in choice and quantity for your table. In any case, it is a simple matter to augment the items that have been served with extra dishes should that be necessary. Warm pita bread is served throughout the meal and you are discouraged from putting much food on your plate. I remember well a tall, handsome waiter called Elie who instructed us on the Lebanese way of eating by just dipping the bread into the various delights. All part of the service. Consequently, the meal is a most friendly affair (akin to a fondu) and best eaten in large groups to provide the best atmosphere. Certainly, this way of eating may occupy several hours and the restaurants place no pressure on you to "hurry along", as it is this aspect of the meal that most of all sets it aside from the trend towards fast food.

A small selection of the many varieties of olives available

17

The style of cooking and eating is famous throughout the Middle East and Greece but the Lebanese seem to have pulled all the strands together by choosing the best dishes for many thousands of kilometres around and renaming it, collectively, as Lebanese food. The Ful is most commonly seen in Egypt, for example, and the stuffed vine leaves in Greece. It is the roundness of the dishes, as an ensemble, that is the most appealing part of the feast.

The strong flavours of the meal dictate the sort of wine that best accompanies it. The most evocative, apt and delicious wine is the Château Musar made by Gaston Hochar in the Bekaa Valley, notorious for warfare and instability over many years. In spite of this, a wonderful, well-aged wine appears in the shops and supermarkets at a very reasonable price. It is a blend of mainly Cabernet Sauvignon with some Cinsault and the blend varies from year to year. When served at a generous room temperature after breathing for a couple of hours, it has a great depth and flavour which stands up really well to the tastes in the food. Other Lebanese wine that I have had has been worse than ordinary. In early visits to the Phoenicia before the Château Musar became available, I remember that a bottle of Chianti seemed to fill the part but in meals at home I would much more go for a robust Australian red such as Chapel Hill Cabernet Sauvignon or an earthy Penfolds Kalimna Bin 28 Shiraz.

The inspiration for the flat bread has come from visits to Greek baker's in Green Lanes, Haringey where there is a huge selection of interesting breads other than the regular pitas. It is an easy matter to flavour the dough simply with oregano and thyme or to throw in even more flavours like olives, garlic and tomato. Once the dough has risen, it can be flattened out and brushed with oil and sprinkled with thyme. The great advantage of a flat loaf is that it can be cut into convenient wedges which are ideal for dipping and dunking. It freezes well, too. Of course, some pita bread, home-made or bought from a baker or supermarket, served warm and soft (a microwave works well for this) is also a great accompaniment.

The meal is set off by the dips: hummus and mutabbal. Although the ingredients are similar, the flavour and texture of these two dishes are subtly different and I never consider them an "either/or". Both of them freeze extremely well and, for ease of thawing out and portion control, you might like to freeze them in ice cube containers. The presentation of these two dips spread out on plates with a dash of olive oil drizzled around the edge of the plate is most attractive. The aubergines for the mutabbal (also known as Baba Ghanoush) may be baked in the oven but are even better cooked over an open flame – the idea of a blow-torch was first given me by my dear friend Ron at The Windsor Lodge Hotel, Swansea back in the 70's and, although I have never tried it, I am sure it would work well. The creaminess and subtle spiciness of this dish contrasts wonderfully with the more grainy texture of the hummus which also has a much more creamy colour. The fact that the word aubergine is derived from a Sanskrit word which means "anti-wind vegetable" suggests that this dish belongs well to a meal which contains chickpeas in two dishes and the ful beans!

Other dips from elsewhere in the book may be incorporated in the array of dishes and, for colour, a pumpkin pâté is an excellent addition. A range of crudités for low-calorie dipping may also be considered e.g. celery, carrots and peppers. It is also a good idea to strain some yogurt overnight by laying a clean J-cloth in a colander over a basin and using the thickened end result in another dip, Labna. Drizzle (once more) a little olive oil over the yogurt "cheese" and sprinkle with powdered dried mint. Alternatively, the Cacik (or Tzatzigi) of yogurt, mint, cucumber and garlic of page 100 of *Vegetarian Dinner Parties* would sit well alongside the other dips.

The Ful Medames is the only dish that should be served warm and so may be a little inconvenient if the buffet is a long-running affair. Also, the dried ful do need overnight soaking and a good couple of hours of cooking to become soft enough to serve. In one of my visits to Auckland, I discovered large tins of these ful beans and, for convenience, used one to make this dish which was extremely well acclaimed. This is a traditional Egyptian dish often served for breakfast accompanied by warm bread and garnished with hard-boiled eggs and tomato. The beans themselves  are hard, small, very dry, brown broad beans. A larger version, gigantes beans, are used later in the book (page 92) and Andreas's Marinated Broad Beans (page 143) are also excellent here.

A bowl of falafels is a great way to greet guests at any event and they are great to dunk into the dips. They are very popular with children and, because they can be fried from frozen, they are great to have as a stand-by in the freezer in case your guests polish them off quickly or in case unexpected guests turn up. Once the mixture is made, it is a relatively mindless task to form the round, compact falafels; a task that can be done in front of a TV. (This is where I find my love of cricket and large-scale food preparation is complementary.) The trays of frozen falafels can be broken up with a strong kitchen slice and they can be stored in plastic bags until required. This is the ultimate, tasty vegetarian fast food when the deep-fried balls are put in an opened-up pita with a shred or two of lettuce and a spoonful of yogurt.

If you have access to fresh vine leaves, then you will be able to make superb stuffed vine leaves. I remember a very hot visit to Adelaide when I stayed in a rented apartment which had vines growing all over the balcony and the "pruning" process resulted in my hostess discovering that she had enough stuffed vine leaves to last her most of the year. I am not sufficiently experienced in using fresh vine leaves from different places to know whether a certain sort of grape type provides better leaves than another; I would be interested in any information on this topic. For most people, particularly in the UK, you will have to rely on the packets of preserved vine leaves packed in brine which are very variable in size and quality. Sometimes you will open a packet and find that all the leaves are large and complete; other times, many leaves will be too small to use, torn and in need of much unfolding. They should be rinsed well before use and, just as for the falafels, the resulting repetitive job of wrapping the leaves can be done while watching a rivetting TV programme or listening to music. If vine leaves cannot be found, then you can use the blanched leaves of a savoy or other loose-leafed cabbage and create a similar tasty

Leon toasts a Lebanese Feast in Balgowlah Heights, the home of Bernard and Julia

dish. It is a sad admission that, due to the time-consuming nature of much of the preparation for this feast (particularly when 500 portions are involved), we did use large tins of stuffed vine leaves at the Fairport Convention Festival in 1997 and they were a fair substitute for the home-made item.

The making of the spinach triangles is another gloriously relaxing job and, for the aforementioned Fairport Festival, a most pleasant day was spent making and freezing these dainties in layers of 24. We placed 5 layers each on bakewell paper in a sturdy lidded box and these kept extremely well in the freezer. For many years I was happy to brush the triangles with olive oil and bake them until golden brown but, since a memorable party in my friends' garden in June '97,

Spinach Triangles

I am convinced that they are even better when fried. The triangles are also wonderful if made with pastry and baked after brushing with oil. The spinach must be well chopped and drained and, for this reason and because it has a great flavour and for convenience, I do like to use tinned spinach once it has been drained well through a fine sieve. Just as the vine leaves vary from packet to packet, so the filo also may drive you mad when the sheets are irregular or are difficult to separate. The Cypressa brand is my favourite, and, because it is lightly floured, it is less likely to dry out while you are using it (unless you have a particularly long distraction).

The Tabbouleh is a salad which is linked heavily with my outdoor catering at festivals as well as being ever present in my buffets for weddings, birthday parties and the like. It is also one that I have demonstrated to many thousands of people who have watched my "Gastronomic Tour of Europe" and "Lebanese Feast" cookery demonstrations. There are many interpretations of the salad but the main essential for me is an abundance of chopped fresh parsley. Now, at festivals, it is not possible to spend many hours involved in the destalking of many boxes of parsley necessary for feeding a multitude of people so I use frozen parsley and this seems to work well, possibly alongside some chopped fresh parsley.

Once the parsley heads are separated from the stalks, the parsley invariably needs a good wash in several changes of water before being drained in a large colander. It can be left overnight unless your kitchen is very warm and then you may not need to spin it before chopping well in a food processor. Any fresh mint to hand can be added at this point and chopped at the same time (although 90% of the time I get by with dried mint). The fine bulgar wheat (or couscous) should be soaked for at least 30 minutes, much longer if possible, in enough water to cover plus an extra centimetre or so. The salad is made spectacularly juicy with lemon juice (fresh if feasible) and the finest Greek Kalamata extra virgin olive oil. Frequently, especially in summer, I add plenty of finely chopped tomatoes or these can be used as a garnish (or use tomato wedges). I have, at various times, used red onions, spring onions and Spanish onions and all are good. Probably my vote would go to the slightly sweeter red onion if I had to choose. The French make a Tabbouleh with little or no parsley, preferring, instead, a mélange of finely chopped salad vegetables. Other ideas that you may find interesting include the addition of some allspice and the use of some chopped preserved Moroccan style lemons (see page 71) instead of some or all of the lemon juice. The Tabbouleh sits prettily on a bed of lettuce leaves garnished with tomatoes as previously described with the addition of some lemon wedges and some fine black olives. Tabbouleh can also be used as part of a huge mixed salad platter as well as being served individually and attractively in round lettuce leaves. It is such a versatile and refreshing salad which improves somewhat for keeping for a day or so and will keep in the refrigerator for up to five days. I have had cause to freeze it and, whilst not advised, it can be used mixed into a fresh tabbouleh. When we make the salad in a dustbin at the festivals, we even have to get by with chopped tinned tomatoes sometimes when labour is short.

The Lebanese plateful at Cropredy, the Fairport Convention Festival of 1997, was completed with a lovely Greek salad of various lettuce leaves, chunks of cucumber, cubes of real Greek sheep's feta cheese, some rocket, basil, watercress, lambs' lettuce, coriander and black olives. With a tasty dressing of red wine vinegar, olive oil (extra virgin, naturally), garlic, sun-dried tomato and herbs, it rounded off a wonderful plateful. Sadly, we prepared only 500 portions and had a queue of 15 people when we ran out of food at 7 pm.

Several other simple meze dishes come to mind if you wish to provide an even larger selection of dishes: you can buy a huge range of olives in many parts of the world often with exotic flavours (cardamom and orange was spotted in Auckland, and the range of North African style olives available in some French supermarkets is quite staggering). For quality and authenticity, the shop to visit is Andreas Michli's in St Anns Road, Tottenham, London. He has some 20 different home-cured styles and sampling before buying is part of the experience of his lovely shop. Other pickled and preserved vegetables such as cucumbers and chillis can be used. Fried or grilled slices of Halloumi are great if a little salty though I do find that it is quite variable and versions of the cheese found in Australia and New Zealand have been disappointing. The brand Chryso is the best that I have found as it is not as salty as some of the others. Halloumi must be eaten soon after cooking as it

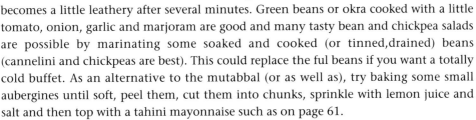

becomes a little leathery after several minutes. Green beans or okra cooked with a little tomato, onion, garlic and marjoram are good and many tasty bean and chickpea salads are possible by marinating some soaked and cooked (or tinned, drained) beans (cannelini and chickpeas are best). This could replace the ful beans if you want a totally cold buffet. As an alternative to the mutabbal (or as well as), try baking some small aubergines until soft, peel them, cut them into chunks, sprinkle with lemon juice and salt and then top with a tahini mayonnaise such as on page 61.

The desserts in Lebanese restaurants are sugary in the extreme which is a great shame. The dish of baby figs in orange juice with a little Greek yogurt and honey is a lovely combination. The baklava is a wonderful dessert when made with a light rosewater syrup and it is simple to prepare. Alternatively, the kaddaifi (shredded filo) filled with ricotta may be preferred or even a dried fruit salad as in *Vegetarian Dinner Parties*. Unusual fresh fruits such as prickly pears are also excellent at the end of a meal with such rich flavours.

This is a marvellous way of eating, particularly on a warm day or evening, simply because the food stands up well to high temperatures. Most of it can be made in advance and kept in the fridge or freezer and, additionally, many of the ingredients can be bought well in advance without fear of deterioration. There are many "tricks of the trade" which will enable you to glamorise or simplify the meal, whichever may be the case and you can prepare just a small selection of the dishes if you are serving a snack meal. Several of the dishes are ideal for a finger food buffet and the meal is equally suited to a friendly sit-down dinner party or a buffet style meal.

Now for the recipes . . .

Greek Flat Bread

1 pkt. easy blend dried yeast	2 tbsps. olive oil
500 g. granary (malthouse) or plain wholemeal flour	salt
	water
1 tbsp. dried oregano	pinch thyme

1 Put all of the ingredients except the thyme into a food processor and blend well.

2 Add sufficient water to make a cohesive but not sticky dough.

3 Wrap the dough in cling film and leave for 30 minutes or so in a warm place.

4 Flatten out the dough into an even disc about 3 centimetres thick. Brush with a little olive oil and sprinkle with the thyme.

5 Bake in a hot oven set at around 200°C, 400°F, gas mark 6 for about 20 minutes until it is turning brown.

6 Cool slightly and serve cut into 12 wedges.

Hummus

125 g. chickpeas, soaked (making 250 g. when well soaked)	120 ml. light tahini
	salt
juice of 3 lemons	60 ml. olive oil
5 cloves garlic	pinch paprika

1 Cook the chickpeas well until soft, in at least twice their volume of water. This will take 30-60 minutes. You may choose to reduce the raw garlic taste in the hummus by cooking the garlic with the chickpeas for the last 15 minutes of their cooking. Roasted garlic is also very good.

2 Put the chickpeas and garlic in the food processor and blend until fairly smooth.

3 Add the lemon juice, olive oil, tahini and salt and blend well. If it is a little stiff and cloying, add a little water, possibly the cooking water from the chickpeas.

4 Keep refrigerated until serving time. Spread the hummus on a large plate and garnish with olive oil drizzled carefully around the edge with a dusting of paprika over the top.

Mutabbal

2 medium aubergines
3 cloves garlic
salt
150 ml. tahini

juice of 3 lemons
up to 1 tsp. chilli
heaped tsp. ground cumin
60 ml. olive oil

1 Bake the aubergines (and garlic with its skin on, if you like) in a hot oven at 210°C, 425°F, gas mark 7 until tender (about 20 minutes. Turn them after 10 minutes). Alternatively, roast them over a flame until the outside is black and the flesh is tender. Cool and remove as much skin as possible.

2 Mix all the ingredients together in the food processor and blend well until completely smooth.

3 As with the hummus, keep it in the refrigerator until you serve it in a similar way on a large flat plate, spread out smoothly, and garnished with olive oil around the edge and black olives, parsley and/or sesame seeds sprinkled over the top.

Ful Medames

200 g. dry ful beans
salt
2 cloves garlic, crushed and finely chopped
60 ml. olive oil

4 tbsps. lemon juice
4 tbsps. parsley
1 tsp. paprika
1 tsp. ground cumin

1 Soak the beans overnight in plenty of water.

2 Boil the beans until tender which may take up to 2 hours.

3 Arrange the beans in a bowl and pour the other ingredients over.

4 Serve warm with chopped fresh parsley or coriander sprinkled over.

Some of the ingredients for the recipes on these pages.
Aubergine, chick peas (dry), chick peas (soaked) and Ful Beans.

Falafels

250 g. chickpeas, soaked
for a minimum of 24 hours
(making about 500 g)

1 medium onion, quartered

2 tsps. ground coriander

2 tsps. ground cumin

4 tbsps. fresh coriander, parsley
or coriander concentrate

salt

2 tsps. baking powder

chilli powder or black pepper, to taste

oil for deep-frying

1 Drain the chickpeas and grind them with the onion in a food processor until you have a fairly smooth paste.

2 Add the other ingredients and blend well.

3 You may leave the mixture in the refrigerator until you want to form the falafels. Make a small walnut size ball and make sure the falafel is compact so that it will not fall apart. You can place the formed falafels on a tray so that they are touching to save space and, if you like, freeze the trayful of falafels. When frozen, you can prise the falafels from the tray and separate them and store in plastic bags in the freezer.

4 Fry the falafels whether frozen or not in hot oil until brown (5 minutes or so). A deep-fat frier does the job particularly well, but you may prefer to shallow-fry, turning the falafels in the oil if necessary.

5 When they are cooked, put the falafels on some kitchen paper to drain or, even better, place them on a bed of finely shredded iceberg lettuce leaves. Serve while still warm, a great snack to offer guests to accompany the first drink of the evening.

Stuffed Vineleaves

12 vineleaves
100 g. cooked brown rice
small onion, finely chopped
1 clove garlic, crushed
2 tbsps. olive oil
half tsp. oregano
half tsp. dill
1 tbsp. tomato purée

1 tbsp. pinenuts
FOR THE COOKING:
1 clove garlic, slivered
4 lemon wedges
white wine
2 tbsps. lemon juice
pepper
2 tbsps. olive oil

1 Fry the onion and the crushed garlic in the olive oil until transparent.

2 Add the rice, herbs, tomato purée and pinenuts and mix.

3 To stuff the vineleaves, first wash off the brine in which they are stored. In the case of fresh vineleaves, just wash them well and drain.

4 Unfold each leaf so that it is flat and place a teaspoonful of the filling on the leaf (either way round) just above where the stem meets the leaf. (Cut off any stem that is still attached)

5 Roll up the leaf to make a nice, neat package: pull the bottom of the leaf over the filling and then fold in the side edges. Then just roll the leaf up as tightly as you can. Note that they do not fall apart while cooking so do not worry about any misshapen stuffed vineleaves.

6 Pack the leaves tightly in an ovenproof dish and put over the lemon wedges, pepper and slivered garlic. In the case of fresh vineleaves, sprinkle over a little salt.

7 Pour over the olive oil, lemon juice and white wine. The liquid will be absorbed or evaporate while the leaves are cooking and they should not become dry.

8 Cover with a lid or some foil and bake at 180°C, 350°F, gas mark 4 for about 25 minutes or cover with clingfilm and microwave for 7 minutes (much longer if you are making a larger quantity for freezing). They are best served cold.

Spinach Triangles

800 g. tin spinach purée, drained well
or 400 g. cooked, chopped spinach

2 tbsps. olive oil

1 medium onion, finely chopped

1 clove garlic, very finely chopped

100 g. feta cheese, cubed

1 tsp. oregano

1 tbsp. pinenuts

pinch ground nutmeg

filo pastry

olive oil for brushing or frying

1 Fry the onion and garlic in the olive oil until transparent.

2 Throw in the spinach, feta, oregano, pinenuts and nutmeg and mix well.

3 Cut the filo pastry into 5 - 6 centimetre strips.

4 Put a teaspoonful of filling near the top of the strip and fold over to form a triangle. Continue folding so that you make a triangle of several layers of filo.

5 Brush each triangle with olive oil and bake at 180°C, 350°F, gas mark 4 for 20 minutes until golden or, better, fry in hot oil for about 5 minutes until an even brown colour.

6 Preferably serve while still warm.

Tabbouleh

60 g. bulgar, soaked in enough water
to cover plus an extra centimetre

half a medium red onion, finely chopped

120 g. parsley, finely chopped

1 tbsp. dried mint
(or 30 g. fresh mint, finely chopped)

salt

100 ml. extra virgin olive oil

100 ml. lemon juice

round lettuce leaves

1-2 tomatoes

6 black olives

lemon wedges

1 Mix the bulgar with the onion, parsley, mint, salt, olive oil and lemon juice.

2 Serve on a bed of lettuce leaves. Garnish the salad attractively with lemon wedges, tomato wedges and black olives. Alternatively finely chop the tomatoes (and more) onto or into the salad and again use the lemon wedges and olives as a final garnish. Mint leaves are good, too.

Kaddaifi

400 g. kaddaif dough
(this is shredded filo)

400 g. ricotta cheese
orange liqueur

melted butter or oil

rosewater syrup (as in Baklava recipe)

2 tbsps. chopped pistachios

1 Separate the kaddaif and put half the dough into a buttered baking dish.

2 Mash the ricotta with a little orange liqueur and spread it over the kaddaif. Add a little grated orange rind, if you like.

3 Put the rest of the dough over the top and brush generously with the melted butter.

4 Bake at 180 C, 350 F, gas mark 4 for 30 minutes or until it is golden.

5 Pour syrup and chopped pistachios over it.

6 While the kaddaifi is still warm, slice it into small squares.

Baby Figs in Orange Juice with Greek Honey & Yogurt

300 g. baby dried figs
orange juice to cover the figs

2 tbsps. Greek honey
4 tbsps. Greek yogurt

1 Soak the figs for a few hours in the orange juice.

2 Poach for 10 minutes over a low flame. Allow to cool.

3 Stir in the honey and yogurt.

4 Serve on their own or with a few pistachios or to accompany one or both of the other desserts.

Baklava

filo pastry
oil or melted butter
500 ml. plain soya milk
250 g. lexia raisins
250 g. dried apricots
400 g. pistachios and/or hazels

FOR THE SYRUP:
5 tbsps. sugar
90 ml. lemon juice
90 ml. rosewater
water
TO GARNISH:
2 tbsps. chopped pistachios

1 Soak the dried fruits in the soya milk (or use some orange juice).

2 Grind the nuts and, separately, the dried fruits. Add sugar and/or cinnamon if you like.

3 Mix the nuts well with the dried fruit.

4 Put a layer of filo into a baking tray and brush with oil or melted butter. Cover with one or two more sheets brushing each in their turn.

5 Spread the filling into the middle of the pastry and cover with the remaining sheets, brushing each with oil or butter.

6 Bake in a hot oven at 200°C, 400°F, gas mark 6 for 15 minutes or so until golden brown.

7 Make the syrup by boiling the sugar, lemon juice, rosewater and some water for 2 minutes. Allow to cool and pour this syrup over the baklava as it is taken out of the oven.

8 Cut the baklava into diamond shaped pieces.

Wood Blewit

*Oyster
Mushroom*

Bay Boletes

Ceps

A beautiful plateful of Chanterelles

Chapter Two

The French Style Dinner Party

here is a great deal of interest in vegetarian food in France and some wonderful restaurants and hotels that cater well for vegetarians, but none is as inspiring as "Le Vieux Moulin" in Bouilland in Burgundy. It is not far from Savigny-lès-Beaune and, as you might imagine, there is a long wine list with a wide choice of wines of the region and helpful advice on the best combination of bottles to accompany your meal. Besides the quaint rural nature of the village with views over hillside meadows, overlooked by some stunning cliffs and the contrasting modern splendour of the hotel annex and attached gymnasium, swimming pool and sauna, the outstanding feature of the hotel is the fantastic food prepared by Jean-Pierre Silva. Each meal is a carefully selected procession of beautifully presented courses, normally eight or nine and over many evenings spent at the hotel, I can scarcely remember a dish being served for a second time to me, with the exception of the most wonderful ceps cooked simply and effectively in butter with garlic and parsley. Much use is made of oils such as hazelnut, walnut and truffle to dress simply cooked baby vegetables, deep-fried herbs such as sorrel and chervil used as garnishes, wild mushrooms collected locally, courgettes and other vegetables cut as spaghetti and home-made bread rolls with a wide variety of flavours such as red wine and, most effectively, nut and sultana to accompany the cheese course. The food is presented on large plates and the whole meal is well planned so that it builds towards a crescendo and yet never leaves you feeling over-full. The cheese board is extensive and there is an impressive array of old brandies to round off the experience. Moreover, the proprietor and his wife are very helpful giving advice, for instance, on local wineries and the best places to go looking for wild mushrooms in the nearby forests. The walks in the forests have resulted in fair numbers of mushrooms being found (mainly ceps, trompettes des morts, chanterelles and coral fungus) which Jean-Pierre was most happy to incorporate in the evening meal.

The wines of the area are world famous and feature the Chardonnay and Pinot Noir grapes. The tasting process is less straightforward than in Australia, for instance, partly because of the language difference but, especially on a second or third visit to the same winery, you will find friendliness and generosity. I have several favourites which rate highly for the tastings, quality of the wine when I open it in England and value for money. First of all, there is Domaine Nudant at Ladoix-Serrigny where simple whites like the "Bourgogne" are inexpensive yet very good while the mid-price Ladoix "Les Gréchons" is an elegant food wine and the "Corton-Charlemagne" is a great white wine, as good as any I have tasted. The reds, similarly, range from good, early drinking blends like the "Bourgogne" and the Ladoix "Les Buis" up to some exceptional Aloxe-Corton wines worthy of many years in the cellar. The tasting is very relaxed and informative by Madame Nudant who has more than a little interest in vegetarian food and an adequate knowledge of English. Moreover, she has been kind enough on several occasions in the past to hold on to boxes of wine from other wineries until we are about to leave the area and, on one occasion, to allow a barrel tasting which is always a privilege. The wines of Maurice Ecard in Savigny-lès-Beaune are also a joy to taste and in the village you should drop in on Parigot & Richard for their Crémant de Bourgogne sparkling wine (Red, Rosé, Crémant Blanc, Blanc de Blanc and Crémant Millésimé). On a good day, you will see the process by which the wine becomes sparkling and be taken to another enchanting cave for the tasting and even friends who have not been greatly enthusiastic about sparkling wine have praised the wines from this maker. They are not expensive and can be used with a dash of a fruit liqueur such as cassis (blackcurrant), framboise (raspberry), pêche (peach), or mûre (blackberry) to make a fantastic pre-dinner drink. In other parts of the Burgundy area I have enjoyed visits to Domaine Jessiaume for an interesting tour of their old caves and excellent white and red Santenay "Les Gravières", Thierry Guyot for a relaxed tasting in a lovely courtyard and some of the better organic wines that I have tasted. Pierre Bourée in Gevrey Chambertin is run by Bernard Vallet whose English is excellent and he sells aged Burgundies from many parts of the region which are wonderful. Beware that the wines have to be labelled so you will have a two hour delay before you can pick them up, time enough to visit the woods near Gilly to find a few wild mushrooms.

It seems a little narrow to pick only one region from a country with such a great gastronomic tradition and, indeed, I have had excellent meals, wine tastings and walks elsewhere in France but, for me, Burgundy has it all. Overnight stops in the Dordogne where there are several good guest houses providing food for vegetarians meant that I discovered the charm of the countryside around the rivers Lot and Dordogne and the town of St Emilion as well as the wines of that area. A friendly and very cheap couple of nights were spent in the Alps at Aspremont enjoying delightful home-made food and spending one day on a 25 kilometre ramble and another cherry picking. Nor should I omit mention of Bernard Loiseau in Saulieu and his wonderful Menu Légumes. As I wrote earlier, there are now many restaurants, hotels and guest houses that cater well for vegetarians but I would still give notice when you are making your booking and give some indication of likes and dislikes.

For me the true flavour of France and the traditions of eating in the French style are to be found only at home and I have been fortunate enough to be gastronomically serenaded as well as instructed over several years in places as far apart as St Pargoire near Montpellier in the South and Brienne-le-Château in Champagne. Meals under Arlette and Ghislain's almond tree in the back garden in the most delightful village of St Pargoire were memorable both for the atmosphere and the food that appeared over a long evening of eating and drinking. I still remember the idea of roasted foil-wrapped vegetables of several types served as a "pot luck" course. Danielle at Brienne introduced

A delightful table setting at the home of Corinne (pictured),
at which many wonderful dinners have been prepared

me to the idea of well aged wines which she had kept for many years in a well-stocked garage and storeroom under the house: Aloxe-Corton, Chablis, Moulin-à-Vent and Alsace wines are just a few that I recall. Her food is based simply on fresh produce from

her garden and the sweetness and richness of her tomato salad with home made mayonnaise (fresh eggs from the hens in the garden) was great. Recently, I have been spoilt by Corinne's hospitality in Imphy, Nevers in central France and dinner parties there have had many points of interest accompanied with wines that go back to 1944. On my last visit, we visited the caves of La Perrière in Sancerre and tasted wine also at the excellent Ladoucette winery in Pouilly. Significantly, for the first dish of this chapter, we ended up in the village of Chavignol and, after tasting some goats cheese at the door we gravitated to the bar where we tasted yet more cheese accompanied by some local white wine and thence we were escorted around the dairy and saw the whole process of making and storing the cheeses. I discovered that the marriage of the local wine with warm goats cheese crottins (small cylinders) served on a bed of oak-leaf lettuce leaves and a simple dressing was one of the great starters. I have since worked on the salad mixture and inserted various garnishes which are, frankly, optional extras to make a simple and effective dish even more glamorous. I have also tried out the salad in Australia and New Zealand with local goats cheese such as Piccolo Chèvre and Wahroonga Chèvre in South Australia and they worked perfectly well. You may allow one chèvre per person depending on the size of the cheese and the appetites of the diners for the cheese or you may slice the cheese before warming into two or three pieces if you wish.

Lena in Adelaide fed me with the idea of toasted walnuts and Bernard in Sydney has long advocated rocket pesto as a very interesting variation on the usual basil version. You may prefer to serve hollowed out cherry tomatoes stuffed with the rocket pesto. The most obvious wine to serve with this is a wine from the Upper Loire such as a Sancerre or a Pouilly Fumé but you may like to look at an aged Hunter River Semillon (Lindemans or Rothbury), a dry and yet fruity Clare Valley Riesling such as Tim Adams or a New Zealand Sauvignon Blanc such as a Montana or a Jackson Estate.

The pumpkin ratatouille is one of several attempts in this book to push this sadly underrated vegetable into a more prominent role in our kitchens. You may like to note the many health advantages of the pumpkin and squash family; good for preventing heart disease, cancer and urinary problems. The seeds also have many advantages for sex and conception, preventing prostate cancer, for stress and mental problems and for fatigue. In Australia you will see many types of pumpkin in even the smallest of greengrocer's and so often have I made this dish in New Zealand as it is a great one to do in a hurry, that my friend Peter has devised a local spelling i.e. ratatui. It would be easy to expand the idea of this dish adding chickpeas to make it more filling and serving it in pastry or on a bed of couscous or rice to make it into a meal in its own right. Now it is much easier to find pumpkin in supermarkets and here in Brentwood we have a farmshop, Crown Corner, which sells 15-20 types of pumpkin and squash including the excellent "Queensland" Blue. I like the idea of combining it in this course with some baby potatoes and even some mushrooms (I have used "hen of the woods") which are flambéed briefly in calvados or brandy and then baked in a cream and cheese sauce. It is, however, very French, so I have been told, to serve each dish as a course on its own.

The pepper custard is a great topping for some wild mushrooms because of its subtle flavour which does not overpower the mushroom flavour. I have used trompettes des morts in this dish and blewits but I feel that ceps are best. The savoury carrot gâteau has some texture which therefore complements the red pepper custard and mushrooms.

I would strongly recommend a cheese course before the dessert because of the range of French cheeses which could be chosen, the lovely rolls to accompany and the need for some food to complement a deep and rich red wine such as a Cabernet Sauvignon. I would choose a Brie de Meaux, Emmental, Reblochon and, perhaps, a goats cheese or a mild blue cheese. Many of the stronger cheeses are better married with a sweet wine.

The apple pie is another excuse to incorporate some calvados into the meal and the walnut cake is a light and delicious dessert. I was told by the owner of a lovely guest house in the Dordogne that they collect the walnuts by waiting for the nuts to fall off the tree and then they have to gather them before the squirrels take their share.

The recipes follow . . .

A Salad of Oak Leaf Lettuce and other green leaves with warmed Goats Cheese, Toasted Walnuts and Slices of Tomato with Rocket Pesto

FOR THE SALAD:
1 oak leaf lettuce (feuille de chêne)
a handful of parsley (Continental)
a few dandelion leaves if young
a few basil leaves

FOR THE CHEESE:
3 or 6 Crottins de Chavignol or
other goats cheese rounds

FOR THE WALNUTS:
100 g. Californian walnuts

FOR THE ROCKET PESTO:
two medium, firm tomatoes

1 bunch (about 100 g.) rocket
70 g. Pecorino Romano
2 cloves garlic
50 g. pinenuts
60 ml. extra virgin olive oil

FOR THE DRESSING:
1 clove garlic
2 tbsps. sherry vinegar
salt
good pinch black pepper
75 ml. extra virgin olive oil

1 Clean the lettuce and other leaves and tear into a large bowl.

2 Cut the cheeses if you are allowing a half per person and put on an oven proof dish wrapped individually or altogether in foil. Place the cheese in a moderate oven at 180°C, 350°F, gas mark 4 for 30 minutes or so (keep an eye on the cheeses as you do not want them to lose their shape or to dry out).

3 Put the walnuts in the oven at the same time as the crottins and toast for about 10 minutes.

4 Grate the Pecorino and blend with all the other ingredients for the pesto i.e. the garlic, pinenuts, rocket and olive oil. Slice the tomatoes thinly and spread generous teaspoonfuls of the pesto on the tomato slices.

5 Blend all of the ingredients for the dressing.

6 Dress the salad and arrange on plates with the tomato slices and toasted walnuts on top. Last of all, place the warm goats cheese on top of the salad ingredients.

It may be a little too much for a starter but you may like to serve a black olive flavoured roll with this to help mop up some of the lovely juices from the salad.

Pumpkin Ratatouille with Flambéed Potato and Mushroom Gratin

FOR THE PUMPKIN RATATOUILLE:

500 g. pumpkin or butternut squash

1 medium aubergine

1 each red and green pepper

1 medium onion

3 cloves garlic

marjoram, basil and/or oregano

800 g. tin tomatoes

olive oil

salt

1 red chilli, finely chopped

1 Cube the vegetables and, if you like, salt the aubergines and leave for a while to allow some of the bitter juices to flow out.

2 Fry the aubergines and peppers separately until just tender and set aside.

3 Fry the onion together with the garlic until transparent. Add the tomatoes, herbs, chilli and pumpkin.

4 When the pumpkin begins to soften, add the fried aubergines and peppers and continue to cook for a short while. Serve warm.

(Add other herbs e.g. savory, thyme as well as tomato purée, courgettes, fennel, celery, leeks etc. according to personal taste and availability).

FOR THE FLAMBÉED POTATO AND MUSHROOM GRATIN:

450 g. small new potatoes, cooked until just tender

250 g. mushrooms ("hen of the woods", oyster or blewits are good)

60 ml. olive oil

60 ml. calvados or brandy

150 ml. double cream

salt

pepper

150 g. Gruyère, grated

1 Fry the mushrooms in the oil for a couple of minutes. Throw in the potatoes.

2 Pour in the calvados or brandy and immediately ignite with a match (or, if you have a gas flame, just shake the pan vigorously).

3 Pour in the cream to put out the flame; it will thicken quite quickly. Season with the salt and pepper.

4 Place in a gratin dish and sprinkle over the cheese. Grill until brown or place in a hot oven for around 15 minutes.

Savoury Carrot Gâteau with Wild Mushrooms cooked in a Red Pepper Custard

FOR THE CARROT GÂTEAU:
600 g. carrots, scraped and cut into
4 cm. lengths
2 medium onions, finely chopped
2 tbsps. olive oil
3 cloves garlic
1 tbsp. agar
100 ml. milk

2 eggs
salt
pepper
2 tbsps. coriander, finely chopped
TO GARNISH:
chervil, finely chopped
handful pinenuts, toasted

1 Steam the carrots for 25 minutes until they are soft.

2 Fry the onions in the oil until transparent.

3 Throw all the ingredients except the pinenuts and a few chervil leaves (for garnish) in a food processor and blend until smooth.

4 Put the mixture into a greased cake tin or cook in individual ramekins. Place the cake tin in a flan dish with a centimetre or so of water and cook, bain-marie, in a hot oven at 200°C, 400°F, gas mark 6 for 40 minutes.

5 Turn out the cake and serve warm, garnished with the pinenuts and chervil leaves.

FOR THE WILD MUSHROOMS COOKED IN A RED PEPPER CUSTARD:

500 g. ceps, trompettes des morts or other wild mushrooms (or a combination)

2 large red peppers, baked in a hot oven until soft

400 g. tin tomatoes

2 medium onions, finely chopped

3 eggs

220 ml. double cream

50 g. butter

1 tbsp. olive oil

salt

pepper

1 Slice the mushrooms and fry in a little olive oil and butter until soft.

2 Fry the onions in the rest of the butter until transparent.

3 Peel the peppers and discard the seeds. Blend well with the onions, tomatoes, eggs, cream and seasonings.

4 In a well-oiled, narrow, oven proof dish (or use a smallish flan dish), place the mushroom at the bottom and the red pepper custard over the top. You may like to sprinkle parmesan or pecorino over the top.

5 Bake, bain-marie, as for the carrot gâteau, in a hot oven at 200°C, 400°F, gas mark 6 for 40 minutes.

6 Serve warm or cold.

Cheeses with Walnut and Sultana Rolls

FOR THE ROLLS:
1 pkt. easy blend yeast
500 g. granary(malthouse) or plain wholemeal flour
75 g. sultanas

50 g. walnuts
2 tbsps. olive oil
salt
water

1 Put all the ingredients except the nuts and water in a food processor and blend well.

2 Add the nuts and blend briefly.

3 Add sufficient water to make a cohesive but not sticky dough.

4 Wrap the dough in cling film and leave for 30 minutes or so in a warm place.

5 Form into small rolls about 4 centimetres across and bake in a hot oven at 200°C, 400°F, gas mark 6 for 13 minutes until brown.

6 Serve while still warm with the cheeses at room temperature.

Tarte aux Pommes and Périgord Walnut Cake

FOR THE TARTE:
400 g. wholemeal flour
1 tbsp. baking powder
200 g. butter
2 egg yolks
sweet white wine
salt

1 kg. cooking apples
50 g. unsalted butter
zest of 1 orange
juice of 1 lemon
50 g. flaked almonds
60 ml. Calvados
50 g. (or more) apricot jam

1 Peel and slice the apples and cook them slowly in the 50 g. butter until soft but not puréed.

2 Mix the flour, baking powder, 200 g. butter, egg yolks, and salt in a food processor and slowly add some sweet white wine (or use cider) until the pastry starts to form a ball.

3 Line a 25 centimetre flan dish with the pastry (roll it out on some Bakewell paper and flick it over into the flan dish). Put the almonds in the pastry case, arrange the apple slices on top and cook for 10 minutes in a moderate oven at 180°C, 350°F, gas mark 4.

4 Combine the orange zest, lemon juice and sugar and warm to dissolve the apricot jam. Pour this over the pie and then flambé with the Calvados (or, if you prefer, include the Calvados when you are cooking the apple slices).

5 Return to the oven for a further 25 minutes until cooked.

FOR THE PÉRIGORD WALNUT CAKE:
6 eggs
250 g. chopped walnuts

60 g. sugar
1 tbsp. baking powder
75 g. crystallised ginger (optional)

1 In a food processor blend well all the ingredients except 50 g. of the walnuts.

2 Throw in the remaining walnuts for a brief time (5 seconds or so).

3 Cook bain-marie style in a medium oven at 180°C, 350°F, gas mark 4 for about 40 minutes.

43

A truly festive Nut Loaf

Chapter Three

A Festive Feast

have met people who tell me that they religiously cook the entire Chapter Ten 'Festive Dinner Party' of *Vegetarian Dinner Parties* each year. I hope that now they will try out some of these new festive dishes which I have demonstrated at my 'Festive' cookery demonstrations in the 90's. Certainly, the range of ingredients commonly available is much greater now than in the early 80's and this chapter reflects my personal campaign for some great foods: wild mushrooms, cranberries, pumpkin and blueberries. I have 'borrowed' a couple of ideas from *Vegetarian Dinner Parties*, simply because I demonstrate the Bircher Potatoes each year and still think that they are unbeatable, and, as an alternative to Christmas Pudding, the Mincemeat and Apple Crumble (with a different topping to that given in the previous recipe) is also difficult to surpass for simplicity and effectiveness.

I have demonstrated a variety of wild mushroom pâtés over the years. I have chosen my favourite one here. Each year I spend many relaxing hours walking in the countryside not more than five kilometres from my home and I find a huge range of edible mushrooms which I preserve in a variety of ways. The very best ones can be put in jars of olive oil (see page 91); otherwise, I fry the sliced mushrooms and stems in butter and/or olive oil and they keep well in the freezer and are great to use in soups, sauces, nutroasts (see page 125) and pâtés. This idea of a baked pâté, not dissimilar from the Carrot Gâteau (see page 40), can easily be extended to other areas and I have successfully done a whole course of baked pâtés. Most of all, the tapenade (see page 102) could easily be varied to include a little cream and some eggs and then baked, as here. The truffle oil is fairly widely available in large supermarkets; it is made with extra virgin olive oil infused with white truffle from Italy and it is my favourite way to use this wonderful ingredient. Just a small amount transforms a dish such as this one (and try it, too, in the Wild Wild Risotto, page 94) and a 250 millilitre bottle will last a long while. Like sesame oil, it is used for flavouring more than as a frying oil and you may prefer to add the truffle oil later in the recipe here and do the frying in butter. The rich flavours of the pâté combine well with the rolls but the nut and cranberry flavours go well also with a cheese course as in chapter two. I would choose a sweetish wine with this course like a Vouvray Moelleux or a light Sauternes.

The quiche has been a favourite at my demonstrations and, particularly, at the festivals for over a decade. I love its richness and crunchiness. It is good when eaten cold (and it can be frozen) but it is different when eaten hot or warm, creamy and oozing blue cheese flavours and smell while still having the nutty texture. Pecans and walnuts work equally well here. It goes well with a lovely mixture of three marinated, grated vegetables. These have colour and, with the marinades, interesting flavours. These will benefit from making well in advance; the flavours are still developing up to three days after having been made. I would drink a French Chardonnay with this course: a Santenay 'Les Gravières' or a Puligny Montrachet would be good.

I am often asked for the recipe for a nutroast. Back comes the reply 'It is not a recipe but a formula: nuts + backing + binding + flavouring = nutroast'. This gives you an infinite range of options. Over the years, I have steamed a nutroast mix in cabbage leaves, included layers of seaweed, made many variations on the theme of layered nutroasts and used ingredients such as mushrooms (see page 125) and sliced oranges to cook at the bottom of the nutroast to decorate and flavour it. Given also that any mix may be formed into burger shapes and fried or into ball shapes and baked, or it may be used to stuff vegetables from peppers and tomatoes to butternut squash and mushrooms, you can see the wide range of possibilities for experimentation. Moreover, many sauces can be devised to complement the flavours of a nutroast.

So, here I have included one of the many successful nutroast recipes (for others, see chapter ten) which cooks well, freezes well and cuts well. Cashews are my favourite nut for a nutroast and I use breadcrumbs most of the time as a backing ingredient. Soya milk does the binding very effectively (and keeps it vegan) and, here, the flavours come from the onions, herbs, orange slices and the stuffing. Although it does microwave well, a good hour in a moderate oven will give you an attractive, brown, crisp finish and it will be delicious with the cranberry sauce.

I give three interesting vegetable accompaniments which I have often demonstrated but I would also refer you to the parsnips in yogurt, sprouts and chestnuts and cauliflower and almonds of Chapter Ten of *Vegetarian Dinner Parties*.

The main course of a festive dinner lends itself to a wide variety of wines: a rich, fruity chardonnay (Lindemans Padthaway), a fine Pinot Noir (Wignalls from Western Australia or a Gevrey Chambertin), or even something heavier like a Chapel Hill Cabernet Sauvignon from South Australia.

The Mincemeat and Apple Crumble with Amaretto was an attempt to give an alternative, lighter dessert to Christmas Pudding. I have nothing against Christmas Pudding; in fact, it is one of my favourite desserts but, unfortunately, it is usually eaten at the time of the year when it can be least appreciated. After a hard day on the stall, be it June, July or August, often with hardly a break for food all day, and with the first chill of evening having an effect (particularly if I am still in my shorts), now <u>that</u> is the time to enjoy a Christmas Pudding, flambéed well in brandy, of course. The Blueberry Gâteau is a much newer idea but it is along the same lines: i.e. a lighter, festive, alternative (but still somewhat alcoholic) dessert. Individual buns could double up and be served to good effect for elevenses or at a tea party. Push the boat out and drink a DeBortoli Noble One Semillon with either of these desserts.

A small gathering of diners enjoy helping Leon research some of the recipes in this book.

Baked Wild Mushroom Pâté

1 clove garlic, finely chopped	2 tbsps. brandy
3 shallots or 1 small red onion, finely chopped	2 eggs
2 tbsps. truffle oil	75 ml. double cream
250 g. wild mushrooms, sliced (bay boletes are best)	salt
	pepper
	2 tbsps. parsley

1 Fry the mushrooms in the truffle oil with the shallots and garlic for about 4 minutes until excess moisture is driven off.

2 Combine all of the ingredients in a food processor and purée to a smooth consistency.

3 Pour the mixture into 6 well-oiled individual ramekins and put them into a flan dish with 2 centimetres of water and cook bain-marie style for 25 minutes at 180°C, 350°F, gas mark 4.

4 Cool and turn out onto a medium size plate. Serve with a few frisée lettuce leaves and the cranberry and pecan flavoured roll.

Cranberry and Pecan Rolls

1 pkt. easy blend yeast	80 g. pecans
500 g. granary (malthouse) or plain wholemeal flour	2 tbsps. olive oil
100 g. dried cranberries	salt
	water

1 Put all the ingredients except the nuts and water in a food processor and blend well.

2 Add the nuts and blend briefly.

3 Add sufficient water to make a cohesive but not sticky dough.

4 Wrap the dough in cling film and leave for 30 minutes or so in a warm place.

5 Form into small rolls about 4 centimetres across and bake in a hot oven at 200°C, 400°F, gas mark 6 for 13 minutes until brown.

Celery, Stilton, Walnut and Port Quiche

FOR THE PASTRY:
200 g. wholemeal flour
1 tbsp. baking powder
100 g. butter
salt
water

FOR THE FILLING:
2 sticks celery, fairly finely chopped
100 g. walnuts (or pecans)
100 g. Stilton
250 ml. single cream (or 50-50 milk and double cream)
3 eggs
30 ml. port

1 Blend the flour with the butter, baking powder and salt. Add the water slowly to make a short crust pastry dough.

2 Roll out the pastry and line a 20 centimetre flan dish.

3 Place the chopped celery in the middle of the pastry case with the walnuts around the outside.

4 Combine the cheese, eggs and cream and pour over the celery and walnuts

5 Using a small jug, pour the port in a spiral over the quiche, starting at the centre.

6 Bake at 180°C, 350°F, gas mark 4 for 25 minutes until brown and set.

Three marinated, grated vegetables

FOR THE CARROTS:
200 g. carrots, grated
2 tbsps. olive oil
2 tbsps. lemon juice
salt
pepper
1 clove garlic, finely chopped

FOR THE BEETROOT:
200 g. beetroot, grated
125 ml. sour cream
2 tbsps. honey
2 tbsps. lemon juice
1 spring onion, very finely chopped
1 clove garlic, finely chopped
salt
pepper
1 tsp. grated horseradish
or 1 tsp. wasabi

FOR THE CELERIAC:
200 g. celeriac, grated
1 pkt. (290 g.) soft tofu
1 clove garlic, finely chopped
2 tbsps. lemon juice
1 tbsp. tamari soy sauce
1 tsp. mustard
salt
pepper

1 In each case, marinate the grated vegetable in the well blended mixture and leave for 12 hours or more.

2 Serve individually, if you like, giving each person a small pile of each vegetable to accompany the quiche. Garnish with some finely chopped parsley, with some pumpkin seeds on the carrot, some sunflower seeds on the beetroot and some black sesame seeds or onion seeds on the celeriac.

Herb and Cashew Nutroast with a Mango Stuffing

2 large onions, finely chopped
75 ml. vegetable oil
400 g. cashews, ground
400 g. breadcrumbs
salt
pepper
2 tbsps. mixed herbs
wine, stock or soya milk

FOR THE STUFFING:
80 g. breadcrumbs
3 tbsps. parsley, finely chopped (or 1 tbsp. dried parsley)
70 g. dried mango (small pieces)
orange juice to cover the mango

2 or 3 orange slices

1 Soak the mango overnight in the orange juice.

2 Fry the onion in the oil until transparent.

3 Combine all the ingredients for the roast and for the stuffing. Use the wine, stock or soya milk to get a firm but somewhat moist consistency.

4 Line a deep, rectangular, oven-proof baking dish with bakewell parchment or greaseproof paper (or use a plastic microwave dish). Lay a couple of orange slices at the bottom and press down well on them a layer of half the cashew mixture. Continue with a layer of the stuffing and complete with the rest of the cashew mixture.

5 Bake at 180°C, 350°F, gas mark 4 for 40 minutes covered and for 20 minutes uncovered. It should be turning golden brown. Alternatively, microwave for 20 minutes on maximum power.

6 Turn it out and slice to serve. It is equally good hot or cold.

Cranberry Sauce

100 g. dried cranberries
100 ml. orange juice or 1 medium orange, seedless and peeled

50 ml. port

1 Simmer the cranberries in the port and orange juice or puréed orange.

2 Blend to your required consistency.

Pumpkin (or Parsnip) Patties or Bake

600 g. pumpkin or butternut
squash (or parsnips)

salt

black pepper

1 tsp. dried sage

pinch ground nutmeg

2 tbsps. wholemeal flour

approx. 100 g. pecorino romano or
a strong flavoured cheese

2 beaten eggs

breadcrumbs

1 Bake the pumpkin for an hour or so in a moderate oven at 180 C, 350 F, gas mark 4 until it is soft and peel and take out the pips when it has cooled, or peel and take out the pips and cut it into cubes and steam for 30 minutes or so until soft (and similarly with the parsnips).

2 Mash the vegetable with a little flour, the seasonings and the cheese to taste.

3 Form the mixture into patties and leave for 30 minutes. Then dip in egg and breadcrumbs and fry in hot oil until golden. Or sprinkle breadcrumbs at the bottom of an ovenproof dish, evenly spread out the mixture and top with more breadcrumbs (brush with beaten egg and/or dot with butter if you wish) and bake for 25 minutes in a moderate oven at 180°C, 350°F, gas mark 4.

Flageolets with Paprika

400 g. tin flageolet beans

1 small onion, finely chopped

3 cloves garlic, crushed and finely
chopped

2 tbsps. olive oil

8 sun-dried tomatoes, soaked
overnight and slivered

2 tsps. paprika

pinch chilli powder

salt

parsley to garnish

1 Fry the onion in the oil until transparent and add the tomatoes and garlic.

2 Add the flageolets, paprika, salt and chilli powder.

3 Serve warm sprinkled with finely chopped parsley. You may like to stir in a tablespoonful of sour cream just before serving.

Bircher Potatoes

**3 large potatoes,
washed but not peeled**

4 tbsps. sunflower oil

1 tsp. caraway seeds

salt

1 Slice each potato into two equal halves.

2 Spread the oil into a baking tray and sprinkle in the caraway seeds and salt evenly.

3 Place the potatoes cut side down in the baking tray and bake at 200 C, 400 F, gas mark 6 for an hour or so until brown on the cut side.

Perhaps include some sprouts and chestnuts or cauliflower with almonds (see *Vegetarian Dinner Parties* p.158).

Mincemeat and Apple Crumble with Amaretto

400 g. mincemeat (see *Vegetarian Dinner Parties* p.160 for a great mincemeat recipe)

3 Bramley apples, peeled and sliced or puréed

100 g. oats

60 g. desiccated coconut

oil

demerara sugar

amaretto

1 Put the apples into a dish and spread mincemeat over them; this is easier if the mincemeat is warmed.

2 Mix the coconut, oats and oil. Include some demerara sugar if you wish. Spread this mixture over the apples.

3 Bake at 180°C, 350°F, gas mark 4 for 20 minutes until brown.

4 Pour amaretto over each portion.

Blueberry Gâteau with a Raspberry Cream Coulis

100 g. unsalted butter

80 g. demerara sugar

3 eggs

80 g. flour

100 g. ground almonds

3 drops vanilla essence

1 tbsp. baking powder

100 g. blueberries (frozen ones are fine)

FOR THE COULIS:

100 g. raspberries (frozen are good for this)

50 ml. framboise (raspberry liqueur)

50 ml. double cream

1 In a food processor, blend the sugar, vanilla, ground almonds, butter and eggs. Blend in the flour and baking powder and mix in the blueberries by hand.

2 Grease a cake tin and fill it with the mixture. Bake at 180°C, 350°F, gas mark 4 for 30 minutes.

3 Bring the raspberries to the boil with the framboise and immediately transfer to a food processor and purée. When cool, stir in the cream.

4 Serve the gâteau, cooled and turned out, on a bed of coulis topped with fresh blueberries, raspberries, wild strawberries and/or redcurrants if you wish.

Chapter Four

A Festive Feast (Cold Menu)

When I do my festive cookery demonstrations at the end of November and early December, I cannot rely on the hall providing me with the facility to serve a lot of hot food and so I am always trying to discover, adapt and invent cold dishes suitable for the festive season when ingredients are sometimes in short supply or expensive. In any case, people always like recipe ideas for the many meals that have to be prepared for the festive period after the main hot meal of Christmas Day. I love to invent new pâtés and dips and, although the wild mushroom pâté is my favourite one to do in November, the three that appear in this chapter give interesting variations of texture and flavour and they combine well with some flavoured breads (and here the number of flavours and combinations of flavours is infinite) as well as other foods that might be provided to dip and dunk, such as pieces of vegetables and corn chips. A good sparkling wine is always popular with this course.

My good friend, Sue Nowak, who has contributed a lovely pudding as a guest recipe in Chapter Twelve, herself asked me for a guest recipe for her book "Hop Cuisine" and I produced a "chicken" and chestnut pie with a beer flavoured jelly poured into the pie after it had been cooked. The first thing to clear up is that this is very much a vegetarian chicken! It is a mushroom that grows sometimes in huge pieces up to 8 kilogrammes and it freezes very well (just as it is). It grows on oak and other trees any time from early summer to autumn. It likes very wet weather and often grows at a considerable height so you will spot me taking a ladder on my country walks. Sue loved the flavours of the filling and the unusual pastry (and I often use Stilton in apple pie pastry) as well as the idea of pouring a beery gelling liquid into the pie to moisten the filling and give it an interesting texture. I have tried the same idea with red wine and feel it is rather more festive and so I present this idea here but do try the beer as well. I love to combine the pie with the sharpness of the salsa with papaya, a fruit which enhances the immune system. A bowl of cranberry sauce would also go well with the pie.

The four salads here feature many flavours and textures. The lentil salad and the pumpkin caponata can be made well in advance which is always an advantage and they can even be frozen. The watercress salad is a great favourite because of its colour and the fact that it incorporates red cabbage, rarely used as a salad ingredient by most people and macadamia nuts which are much loved by nearly everyone who is lucky enough to have tried them. The potato salad has similar merits of colour, texture and interesting flavours and a dairy-free mayonnaise with character is a feature.

Finally, since I discovered dried cranberries and their great health benefit in keeping our waterworks in good order, I have tried to incorporate them in as many dishes as possible, sweet and savoury. A fresh fruit salad may lack colour – add some cranberries. No blueberries available for your white chocolate cheesecake (page 148) – use cranberries. Cranberry bread with a cheese board works well, so try a bowl of cranberries with cheese and celery (and save a few calories!). In this chapter you will find a juicy baklava which is easy to make from soaked cranberries and mincemeat. This is a different festive dessert which has been very popular at my demonstrations and buffets that I have done in the run up to Christmas.

A fine specimen of Chicken of the Woods, growing on an oak tree in Brentwood

Capriata

400 g. cooked cannelini beans
2-4 cloves garlic, cooked with the beans
salt

40 ml. red wine vinegar
chilli powder to taste
50 ml. extra virgin olive oil

1 Put all of the ingredients in a food processor and blend until smooth.

2 Garnish with a very light dusting of chilli powder.

Aubergine and goats cheese pâté

1 large aubergine, baked until soft
(20-30 minutes in a hot oven)

4 cloves garlic, baked in skins with
the aubergines (but for 10 minutes
only)

100 g. soft goats cheese

3 tbsps. extra virgin olive oil
1 tsp. ground cumin
1 tbsp. fresh coriander (or use
1 tsp. dried coriander - the herb,
not the spice, or 1 tsp. coriander
concentrate)

salt (if required)

1 Peel the aubergine when cool and blend with the peeled garlic and all the other ingredients until completely smooth.

2 Garnish with a sprig of parsley or chervil.

Artichoke and walnut pâté

12 pitted black olives
1 clove garlic, roasted for 10
minutes in a hot oven

250 g. artichoke hearts (marinated,
or tinned. If fresh, discard the outer
leaves and choke and boil for 10-20
minutes depending on size)

1 tbsp. capers
a dozen or so good basil leaves
100 g. Californian walnuts, toasted
1 tbsp. brandy
3-4 tbsps. walnut oil

1 Blend all the ingredients together until well mixed but leave some scaly texture from the artichokes and some crunchiness from the walnuts.

2 Garnish with alternate carrot and celery sticks ready to dip.

Sun-dried tomato, garlic and basil flavoured flat bread

1 pkt. easy blend yeast

500 g. granary(malthouse) or plain wholemeal flour

a dozen or so sun-dried tomatoes, soaked overnight in water (or wine)

2 cloves garlic

a dozen or so basil leaves (or 2 tsps. dried basil)

2 tbsps. olive oil

salt

water

1 Put all the ingredients except the water in a food processor and blend well.

2 Add sufficient water to make a cohesive but not sticky dough.

3 Wrap the dough in cling film and leave for 30 minutes or so in a warm place.

4 Form into a flat disc about 3 centimetres thick and bake in a hot oven at 200°C, 400°F, gas mark 6 for 20 minutes until brown.

Black Olive Flavoured Flat Bread

Follow the instructions for the previous recipe but substitute 100 g. pitted black olives for the tomatoes, garlic and basil and leave out the salt. You may also choose to omit the olive oil.

Some flat braed loaves

"Chicken" and Chestnut Pie

FOR THE PASTRY:
120 g. Stilton or other blue cheese
300 g. flour
1 tbsp. baking powder
100 g. butter
3 spring onions
egg to glaze

FOR THE JELLY:
100 ml. red wine
2 tsps. agar

FOR THE FILLING:
1 large onion, finely sliced
80 g. butter or use sunflower oil
200 g. "chicken" of the woods
(Laetiporus Sulphureus), finely
sliced or 400 g. other mushrooms

150 g. chestnuts, cooked and peeled
or dried chestnuts (rehydrated
weight)

half a medium red pepper,
quartered and finely sliced

1 tsp. grated horseradish
100 g. sweetcorn
dash Worcester sauce or soy sauce

1. For the filling, fry the onion in the butter for a short while and throw in the mushroom and red pepper.

2. Add the chestnuts, horseradish, sweetcorn and Worcester sauce and season further with salt and pepper if you wish.

3. Mix the ingredients for the pastry in a food processor and enough water or milk to make a dough.

4. Roll out a pastry case and fill with the mushroom mixture. Roll out a top for the pie and seal well.

5. Glaze by brushing with beaten egg and bake in a hot oven at 200°C, 400°F, gas mark 6 for 25 minutes.

6. Warm the red wine (or use real ale) with the agar until it has dissolved. Do this shortly before you need to use it.

7. Take the pie from the oven when brown and crisp and allow to cool slightly. Pour the red wine and agar mixture slowly and carefully into the filling of the pie by using a small funnel.

8. Serve warm or cold with the Papaya Salsa.

Papaya Salsa

1 ripe papaya, peeled and de-seeded
1 small red onion
juice of a lime

handful coriander leaves
1 small red chilli, de-seeded
salt

1 Put all the ingredients on a large chopping board and chop with a large knife until the salsa is reasonably smooth and very well mixed. Doing this by hand rather than with a food processor means that the salsa will have some texture.

2 Serve in a bowl with the pie.

Red Cabbage and Watercress Salad with a Hot Orange Marinade

200 g. red cabbage, finely shredded
(or use red chicory for a very
special effect)

large bunch watercress, washed
and with most of the stalks taken
off

80 g. roasted and salted
macadamias (or use roasted hazels)

FOR THE MARINADE:
80 ml. extra virgin olive oil
juice and rind of 2 large oranges
salt
1 tbsp. red wine vinegar
pinch caraway seeds

1 Arrange the red cabbage, watercress and nuts in a salad bowl.

2 Heat the orange juice and rind in the oil and add the vinegar and caraway seeds. Cook to reduce for 10 minutes.

3 Pour the dressing over the other ingredients and serve immediately.

Marinated Puy Lentil Salad

250 g. cooked puy lentils
1 medium onion, finely chopped
2 sticks celery, finely chopped
1 courgette, finely chopped
1 large carrot, finely chopped
100 g. dried cranberries
3 tbsps. olive oil
FOR THE DRESSING:
2 tbsps. parsley
salt
pepper

2 tbsps. balsamic vinegar
3 cloves garlic
80 ml. extra virgin olive oil
FOR THE GARNISH:
1 red pepper, roasted until soft, peeled, de-seeded and cut into thin slices
a few red basil leaves
a few thin slices parmesan (Reggiano)
a few green olives

1 Drain the lentils well.

2 Fry the finely chopped vegetables in the olive oil until soft.

3 Combine the lentils, vegetables and cranberries.

4 For the dressing, blend the garlic, parsley, salt, pepper, and balsamic vinegar. Add the olive oil gradually until you have a thick dressing. Stir this into the lentils and leave for several hours.

5 Serve in a bowl garnished with the red pepper slices, red basil leaves, parmesan and green olives.

Potato and Broccoli Salad with a Tahini Mayonnaise

450 g. small potatoes, cooked until tender
200 g. raw mushrooms
250 g. broccoli florets, cooked for no more than 5 minutes
100 g. macadamias
FOR THE DRESSING:
100 ml. tahini

1 clove garlic
salt
75 ml. lemon juice
2 tbsps. parsley
pepper or chilli powder (to taste)
100 ml. olive oil
water if required

1 Combine all the ingredients for the dressing and add enough water to create a mayonnaise-like consistency.

2 Combine all the ingredients for the salad and mix in the dressing.

Pumpkin Caponata

350 g. pumpkin or butternut
squash, cubed

75 ml. olive oil

2 tbsps. sultanas

salt

2 sticks celery, coarsely chopped
(or use the same quantity of
fennel)

400 g. tin tomatoes

100 g. green olives

60 g. capers

50 ml. red wine vinegar

1 Put all the ingredients into a saucepan and simmer for 20-30 minutes until the pumpkin is soft.

2 Serve warm or cold, possibly garnished with a few toasted pinenuts. You may like to add aubergines, peppers or courgettes. Also, the addition of some sun-dried tomatoes at the end of the cooking will enhance the flavour and absorb some of the juices.

Mincemeat and Cranberry Baklava

450 g. mincemeat

100 ml. port

200 g. dried cranberries

filo pastry

50 g. melted butter

50 ml. orange juice

50 ml. amaretto

1 Mix the mincemeat, port and cranberries. Add a few pinenuts if you like. Mix well and leave for an hour or so.

2 Place a layer of filo at the bottom of an ovenproof dish and brush with melted butter. Fill the pie and top with several sheets of filo, brushing each with more butter.

3 Cook for 20 minutes at 200°C, 400°F, gas mark 6 or until the filo is crisp and brown.

4 Mix the orange juice and amaretto and pour over the pie as soon as it has left the oven.

Chapter Five

A Dinner for Phil

hen you mention that you are cooking a vegetarian gourmet meal with no garlic, leeks, onion or chives, the common reaction is: "What can you cook, then?". Not only can a great meal be constructed with such a restriction, but it is, arguably, the most glamorous array of dishes in this book. Moreover, there are dishes elsewhere which would also fulfil the criteria of this chapter and others that can easily be adapted. Equally, you may like to incorporate some onion or garlic into some of the dishes of this chapter. Phil is a very healthy and extremely fit man but he has severe allergic reactions if he eats any member of the allium family. As you will see if you prepare this meal, this is not a problem.

Phil

The nori seaweed rolls can be varied in many ways but they are a most attractive and tasty way to eat a very healthy ingredient that softens and moistens when rolled around cooked rice. The Sushi rice is treated so that it sticks together when cooked. It is easier to form the rolls with this special ingredient but short grain rice can also be used. Any selection of shredded vegetables may be used in the filling but the pickled ginger is particularly good. The traditional way of rolling them up is to make a cylinder, pure and simple, but I prefer to wrap the seaweed around the rice so that it completely surrounds the rice filling. Then the nori rolls are left to soften in a cool place, well wrapped in clingfilm and cut in half or in smaller pieces and served with a small bowl of dipping sauce. It is a perfect entrée, great with a glass of Semillon (I recommend the Amberley from W. Australia).

I was very pleased to have adapted one of my all time favourite recipes, the onion bhaji, into a new form suitable for this dinner party. Fennel can be slivered up in just the way required for an onion bhaji and it goes extremely well with orange and so the idea of a fennel fritter similar to an onion bhaji was born. Dipped into a delicious orange sauce, they are exceptionally tasty.

The next two dishes feature delicate and interesting combinations of flavours and both look most attractive on the plate. They could even be combined if you surround the tower with the pumpkin topped with the tomato sauce. The delicate theme is

63

continued with the courgette flowers. Italians stuff the courgette flowers with mozzarella, coat them in a light batter and fry in hot olive oil. In this way they must be consumed immediately. In any case, they are a gorgeous, delicate luxury which would glamorise any meal.

The couscous is remarkably good if you add a few chickpeas for texture and some finely chopped parsley and preserved lemons for flavour. Finally, you can turn the dish into a work of art by arranging over the top an attractive range of oven roasted vegetables and herbs; any combination is possible to create a pretty picture. We are now approaching the part of the meal where a bottle of light red such as a Gigondas or a New World Grenache would fit the bill.

It is unlikely that you will have the 'energy' to eat both the pasta and the stuffed champagne pancakes; both are tasty main course dishes with exotic ingredients. I have tried many flavoured pastas, some very expensive but only two at all effective. One was red chilli flavour which certainly had a distinct flavour. The other was also found in a most interesting shop called The Five Star Gourmet in Crows Nest, Sydney where native ingredients or 'bushtucker' is found. The flavour was lemon myrtle and I have always brought back quantities to use in my home-made pasta. It comes from a rainforest tree from the east coast of Australia and releases a tempting combination of taste and aroma similar to the blend of sweet lemon grass, lemon and lime oils. It is supposed to be good in soups, sauces, fruit stews and pickles and in making herb butter or custard. I have used it only in this pasta where it is excellent, particularly when the pasta is coloured green with the addition of parsley (or use another herb). The pasta looks attractive on a bed of red pepper sauce which is along the lines of the aubergine and pepper pâté from *Vegetarian Dinner Parties* and the flavours are complementary. Some extra mushrooms cooked into the pasta and plenty of parmesan finely sliced over the pasta make it even more glamorous.

It was my great friend, Bernard, who introduced me to the idea of champagne pancakes using Australian sparkling wine rather than milk. They are very good and here they are wrapped around a stuffing of puréed celeriac with a rich blue cheese sauce which would suggest a red wine from Mercurey or Santenay. Make an extra batch of these pancakes because they are very good to freeze.

The Australian connection continues because there, in delis, quince paste is commonly found. I was about to make a pecan pie for Bernard when he suggested I use his quince paste in the filling. I was unsure that it would work as I had usually used honey or corn syrup (or even maple syrup) but I gave it a go and it did work; a crunchy, rich and dangerously moreish dessert – beware!

Couscous with Oven Roasted Vegetables (page 71)

Sushi

360 g. Sushi rice, cooked
3 cooked shiitake mushrooms, cut into thin strips
1 medium carrot, finely shredded
half a red pepper, finely shredded
a small piece cucumber, finely shredded

6 nori sheets
a few pieces pickled ginger
FOR THE DIPPING SAUCE:
3 tbsps. seasoned rice vinegar
3 tbsps. tamari soy sauce
1 tsp. wasabi powder
2 tbsps. sesame oil

1 Place a nori sheet diagonally in front of you and spread about 2 tablespoons (60 g.) of the rice on the sheet about 5 centimetres from the corner in a cylinder about 6 centimetres across.

2 Place on top of the rice some of each of the vegetables and the pickled ginger (or reserve the ginger for garnish).

3 Roll the nori sheet up from the bottom corner over the filling and fold in the corners. Then continue to roll to make a neat and tight cylinder. Some people find this easier using a special sushi mat.

4 Cover the rolls with clingfilm or wrap individually in clingfilm and store in the refrigerator until you serve.

5 Using a very sharp knife, cut the sushi into several slices and arrange on a plate. A small piece of pickled ginger in the centre of each sushi piece is most attractive.

6 Either pour the dipping sauce over the sushi or, if they are holding together well, invite guests to help themselves by hand and dip them into the dipping sauce made by combining all the ingredients. Beware the wasabi (which is also available as a paste in a small tube).

Fennel Fritters with an Orange Sauce

1 large head fennel, shredded
oil for deep-frying

FOR THE BATTER:

150 g. gram (chickpea) flour
(besan)

grated rind and juice of 2 large
oranges

1 tsp. fennel seeds, ground

salt

1 tbsp. baking powder

FOR THE SAUCE:

60 g. butter

2 tbsps. wholemeal flour

grated rind and juice of 2 large
oranges

salt

pepper

cinnamon (optional)

1. Mix the ingredients for the batter using a little white wine if necessary to obtain a thick batter which will adhere to the fennel.

2. Mix in the fennel and drop tablespoons of the mixture into the hot oil until brown.

3. For the sauce: melt the butter in a pan and add the flour to make a roux.

4. Slowly add the orange juice and season well. You could also add a little white wine.

5. Add the orange rind and cook until well mixed and thick.

6. Serve the fritters with a central bowl of sauce for guests to dunk their fritters.

Sushi

Marinated Pumpkin with a Sun-dried Tomato Topping

FOR THE PUMPKIN:

450 g. grated pumpkin (butternut squash is best)

100 ml. extra virgin olive oil

50 ml. balsamic vinegar

salt

pepper

1 tbsp. chervil, finely chopped

FOR THE DRESSING:

250 g. ricotta cheese

1 tbsp. basil, finely chopped

12 sun-dried tomatoes, soaked overnight

pepper

TO GARNISH:

a few pumpkin seeds

1 Combine all the marinade ingredients together and pour over the pumpkin. Leave for 12 hours or more.

2 Blend the ricotta with the tomatoes, basil and pepper.

3 On individual plates, on a bed of rocket, dandelion leaves, radicchio or frisée if you like, arrange small piles of the pumpkin with a generous amount of the topping. Sprinkle with pumpkin seeds to garnish.

Tower of Fried Aubergines, Mozzarella, Basil and Sun-Dried Tomato

1 large aubergine
2 eggs, beaten
250 g. breadcrumbs
olive oil for frying
1 mozzarella (buffalo milk is the best)

6 basil leaves (or a thin layer of creamed basil)

6 sun-dried tomatoes, soaked overnight in water

1 Slice the aubergines fairly thinly and sprinkle with salt. Leave for 30 minutes to drain.

2 Dip the aubergine slices in egg and breadcrumbs and fry in the olive oil until golden and crisp.

3 Arrange the tower of slices of aubergines, basil, mozzarella (thinly sliced), and sun-dried tomato, whole or slivered.

4 Finish off with a final aubergine slice. You could introduce other layers such as plain or, better, egg, breadcrumbed and fried polenta slices and it could be served on a bed of peppers in olive oil (see *Vegetarian Dinner Parties* p. 44). A little truffle oil or white truffle sauce over the top is another successful extension to this idea.

Stuffed Courgette Flowers

12 courgette flowers (they
normally come with the small
courgettes attached)

40 g. pinenuts

40 g. soft breadcrumbs

a few cooked, chopped wild
mushrooms

a little white wine to moisten the
mixture

salt

pepper

2-3 tbsps. hazelnut oil

1 Open up the flower and carefully take out the hard central piece inside
(the pistil, I believe).

2 Blend the pinenuts, breadcrumbs, mushrooms and a little white wine. A couple of
leaves of tarragon could be included.

3 With a small spoon or just with your fingers push as much filling into the flower
hearts as is sensible and lay them on an ovenproof plate.

4 Sprinkle with salt and pepper and brush with hazelnut oil. Bake in a moderate oven
at 180°C, 350°F, gas mark 4 for 12 minutes. Serve with the rest of the oil poured
over.

Couscous with Oven Roasted Vegetables

150 g. couscous, soaked overnight
in enough water to cover
(preferably wholemeal couscous)

150 g. cooked chickpeas

1 Moroccan preserved lemon,
finely chopped

3 tbsps. extra virgin olive oil

2 tbsps. parsley, finely chopped

3 tomatoes

6 pieces asparagus (or use green
beans)

1 courgette

1 red pepper

12 baby carrots

olive oil

salt

pepper

balsamic vinegar

a few toasted pinenuts

1 Mix the couscous with the chickpeas and the lemon pieces. Add the parsley and olive oil and adjust the seasoning.

2 Halve the tomatoes and slice the other vegetables where necessary. Brush with olive oil and balsamic vinegar and sprinkle with salt and pepper. Roast in a moderate oven at 180°C, 350°F, gas mark 4 for 45 minutes until they are soft. Check them from time to time as their rates of cooking will depend on their size. If Phil was not coming to dinner, some roasted garlic would be good.

3 Arrange the couscous on an attractive salad platter and arrange the vegetables attractively on top. Sprinkle over the pinenuts. Some harissa would be an exciting accompaniment (but it has garlic in it!).

To preserve lemons:
Cut lemons into wedges and salt well. Leave in a warm place for 6 weeks and then top with vegetable oil. Use in any recipes where a lemony flavour is required, e.g. Andrew's Siny'et Bedingal on page 145.

Lemon Myrtle Pasta on a Red Pepper and Aubergine Sauce

FOR THE DOUGH:

250 g. pasta flour (more if necessary)

3 eggs

salt

1 tsp. lemon myrtle leaves, powdered (or use 1 tsp. grated lemon rind)

1-2 tbsps. chopped parsley

FOR THE SAUCE:

2 red peppers, baked until soft in a hot oven (about 15 minutes, turn halfway through)

1 medium aubergine, baked until soft (20 minutes or so, turn again)

2 tbsps. lemon juice

2 tbsps. extra virgin olive oil

2 tbsps. crunchy peanut butter

freshly ground black pepper

1 Make the dough in the food processor with all the ingredients. Add more flour if necessary to make a dry but cohesive ball. Allow to rest in the refrigerator for an hour or so wrapped in clingfilm.

2 Peel the peppers and aubergines and discard the seeds from the peppers. Purée all the ingredients for the sauce and add more olive oil if necessary for the right pouring consistency.

3 Take walnut size balls of the pasta and make a thin sheet with a pasta maker. Allow it to dry for a short while on a clean tea towel and then cut it into thin noodle-shaped strips. Flour lightly so it does not stick together, or, preferably, throw it immediately into plenty of boiling salted water for 2-3 minutes.
It can be re-heated in the micro-wave and served on a bed of the sauce. Parmesan or some marinated wild mushrooms would be good to throw over the top.

Stuffed Champagne Pancakes with a Blue Cheese Sauce

FOR THE PANCAKES:
300 ml. sparkling wine
160 g. sifted wholemeal flour
4 eggs
salt
pepper
oil for frying
FOR THE FILLING:
1 kg. celeriac and/or carrots, steamed or boiled until tender
100 g. blanched almonds

50 ml. double cream
pinch nutmeg
FOR THE SAUCE:
50 g. butter
2 tbsps. wholemeal flour
200 ml. milk
vegetable stock to adjust the consistency
100 g. blue cheese (Roquefort is best)
2 tbsps. port

1 Combine the ingredients for the pancakes and allow to rest for an hour or so.

2 Meanwhile prepare the pan: put plenty of salt into it and heat until the salt begins to darken. Discard the salt. Now the pan will truly not stick.

3 Fry the pancakes in a little oil and store with greaseproof paper in between. These will keep well in the refrigerator or freezer so it is worth making large quantities for future use.

4 Mash the root vegetables (parsnips or pumpkin may be included) and add cream, nutmeg and other seasonings if you wish. Stir in the almonds.

5 For the sauce, melt the butter in a pan and stir in the flour to make a roux.

6 Slowly pour in the milk and the stock including some white wine if you like.

7 Cook slowly until the sauce begins to thicken.

8 Stir in the crumbled pieces of blue cheese and the port.

9 Wrap the pancakes around the filling and pour the sauce over them. (Cranberry sauce "watered" down with lots of port would be a possible alternative to this rich cheese sauce).

Pecan Pie with Quince Paste

300 g. wholemeal flour
100 g. butter
grated rind of one orange
1 tbsp. baking powder
water and/or orange juice

300 g. pecans
200 g. quince paste
5 eggs
70 ml. orange juice
crystallised ginger (optional)

1 Mix the flour with the butter and add in the orange rind and baking powder. Add enough water and/or orange juice to make a short crust pastry.

2 Bake the pastry case blind in a hot oven at 200°C, 400°F, gas mark 6 for 8-10 minutes. Put some greaseproof paper and some old beans on top to avoid "blisters" forming.

3 Spread the pecans and chopped ginger if used into the pastry case.

4 Blend the eggs, orange juice and quince paste (or use honey, maple syrup or corn syrup). Pour this over the pecans and bake in a lower oven at 180 C, 350 F, gas mark 4 for 30 minutes until brown and set. Serve hot or cold with or without cream.

A typical Onion and Garlic stall in France – but you won't find Phil here!

Chapter Six

A 'Sticky' Dinner

his idea was born in Adelaide after visiting some wineries and tasting some excellent 'stickies', or sweet white wines. I realised that, although I had tasted some fine sweet wines, particularly while staying in France, my brain and tastebuds were always so jaded at the time that I sampled them that I had no concept of their quality or how they matched the food that accompanied them. It was obvious that lovely botrytis Rieslings and Semillon that I had just tasted would well accompany certain savoury dishes and cheeses and I began the task of finding a well rounded menu that would be amenable to different sweet wines with every course. This has not been the easiest research that I have attempted because of a lack of understanding of the power of sweet wines in the general population as well as in the wine outlets that I approached for advice and to purchase the wines that I hoped would work. Moreover, the complete seven or eight course dinner party with a range of sweet wines was a gastronomic extravaganza and it required will power to carry the

A delicious dessert (see page 86)

research on to the end. The common belief of the guests who helped me with this exercise was that a selection of the dishes would have sufficed, a lemon sorbet in the middle of the meal would have invigorated a flagging palate and that this chapter may be used much more to select a dish to include in a more varied dinner party than as a dinner party in its own right. Because the dishes are distinctive and have interesting characteristics, I will leave it to you to decide whether you keep religiously to the format of the chapter or lighten the load on the guests by incorporating something lighter like a salad with a fruity dry wine.

The onion bread was based on the idea of pull-apart bread that I saw in Sydney and was cemented in my mind by a lady on a cookery course that I was running in Milton Keynes. When served straight from the oven, it will fall apart but it would be good if served in wedges; it is a bit like a cake in any case. The sweetness of the slow-cooked onions is a wonderful flavour to complement the richness of the pâté and any extra bread will be good to have with the soup or a cheese course (Taleggio is a great cheese with this bread). Vic-Bilh is from the very South West of France and this is a fresh tasting fairly sweet wine. The Recioto di Soave is a very approachable wine and a delightful accompaniment to the first course.

The idea for something spicy was a logical follow-on from the advice that the botrytis Rieslings accompany South-East Asian food extremely well. Indeed, this was the easiest and best match of food with wine. The wonderful depth of flavour of the soup suggests that it would be an excellent sauce with pasta, particularly ravioli. The alternative pumpkin soup could be spiced up but its simplicity is its appeal and it can be served most attractively in the shell of the pumpkin. Cheese and potatoes are both common additions to a pumpkin soup and a light sherry goes well with it.

The Champagne Pancakes would be good if made with leeks rather than with asparagus. The use of wholemeal flour in making the pancakes undoubtedly means that they will be thicker and, therefore, heavier than if made with white flour. The two Loire wines which superbly accompany the asparagus and tarragon flavours are made with the Chenin grape affected by noble rot which concentrates the sweetness of the grapes. The German wine is an example of a well made, fruity, German wine that is extremely good value for money.

The sweet onion tartlets have such a delicious richness and creaminess that it is a great surprise that the finest wine that was found to accompany them was a most inexpensive Californian wine from the Napa Valley.

If you reach the dessert stage of the meal with three desserts to taste and little appetite remaining then you may decide to serve them as one course The unfortunate drawback of this would be the loss of effectiveness of the wonderful Recioto della Valpolicella, a sweetish red wine, as a superb accompaniment for the raspberry mousse. The Tira Mi Su goes well with the two rich Orange Muscat wines from California and Victoria and the Macadamia Tart with the berry flavours of the blueberries would be enhanced by a bottle of Elysium Black Muscat made by Andrew Quady, the winemaker responsible for the Essensia. His Starboard is also an exciting proposition with a varied cheeseboard.

Some of the sweet wines mentioned in this Chapter

Onion and Cheese Loaf

**1 large sweet onion, thinly sliced
and fried in butter as for the tart**

1 pkt. easy blend dried yeast

**500 g. granary (malthouse) or
plain wholemeal flour**

2 tbsps. olive oil

1 tbsp. salt

water

80 g. grated cheddar cheese

1 Put all of the ingredients except the onion and cheese into a food processor and blend well.

2 Add sufficient water to make a cohesive but not sticky dough.

3 Wrap the dough in cling film and leave for 30 minutes or so in a warm place.

4 Press half the dough into a loaf tin and spread the onion over the top and then push in the rest of the dough. Alternatively, flatten out the dough and spread the onion on top then roll up as for a roulade. Sprinkle over the cheese.

5 Bake in the middle of a hot oven set at around 200°C, 400°F, gas mark 6 for about 25 minutes until it is turning brown.

Chestnut, Celeriac and Gorgonzola Pâté

**250 g. chestnuts, shelled and
cooked**

250 g. celeriac, cooked until tender

250 g. Gorgonzola

8-10 strands saffron

2 tbsps. coriander leaves

2 tbsps. brandy

salt

good pinch pepper

FOR A GARNISH:

20 g. toasted pinenuts

1 Mash the celeriac and chestnuts with the blue cheese and reheat in the microwave until the mixture bubbles.

2 Add the saffron and other ingredients and blend well.

3 Serve in individual dishes garnished with toasted pinenuts (toasted either in a pan over a medium flame for 2-3 minutes or in a moderate oven for 5-6 minutes) and, possibly, with some deep-fried chervil leaves.

[recommended wines: Pacherenc du Vic Bilh Moelleux, Recioto di Soave]

Spicy Tomato Soup

2 tbsps. sunflower oil
half tsp. cumin seeds
half tsp. fennel seeds
half tsp. mustard seeds
small red chilli
2 tbsps. gram (chickpea) flour
1.5 kg. tomatoes, peeled and chopped (or use tinned tomatoes)

2 tbsps. tomato purée
handful red basil leaves (or use green leaves)
salt
100 ml. double cream (optional)
1 tsp. demerara sugar
3 tbsps. brandy

1 Fry the whole spices in the oil for a minute or so. Do not burn the spices.

2 Stir in the gram flour to make a roux.

3 Stirring continuously, pour in the tomatoes and add about 250 ml. water. Stir in the tomato purée.

4 Let the mixture simmer for about 30 minutes stirring occasionally and add the basil leaves and salt. Blend well until very smooth.

5 In another saucepan, heat the cream (if used) with the sugar to the point of boiling and add this slowly into the soup which must be off the boil. Alternatively, stir the sugar into the soup.

6 Add the brandy and serve.

[recommended wine: Lindemans Botrytis Riesling]

A selection of pumpkin and squash at a small greengrocer's in Balgowlah near Sydney

81

Pumpkin Soup

1 small round pumpkin,
2 shallots, finely chopped
30 g. butter
700 ml. vegetable stock and/or
medium white wine

salt
plenty of pepper
2 tbsps. double cream
2 tbsps. lemon juice

1 Cut off the top of the pumpkin and take out the pips. Hollow out as much flesh as possible using a spoon.

2 Fry the shallots in the butter until soft and add the pumpkin flesh.

3 Continue to cook for a few minutes, stirring frequently.

4 Add the stock or wine and seasonings and simmer for 25 minutes.

5 Blend well and add the cream and lemon juice.

6 Pour the soup back into the pumpkin shell and serve immediately.

[recommended wine: Pale Cream Sherry]

Champagne Pancakes with Asparagus and a Tarragon Sauce

FOR THE CHAMPAGNE PANCAKES
(see page 73)
FOR THE FILLING:
24 stems asparagus
salt
FOR THE SAUCE:
50 g. butter
100 g. shallots, very finely chopped
30 g. wholemeal flour

300 ml. milk
salt
pinch pepper
pinch grated nutmeg
60 g. Gruyère cheese
1 tbsp. tarragon, finely chopped
1 tbsp. chervil, finely chopped
1 tbsp. lemon juice

1 Make the pancakes as previously described.

2 Boil the asparagus in salted boiling water for 8-10 minutes until tender but firm. Drain the stalks and set aside.

3 To make the sauce: fry the shallots in the butter until softening and add the flour. Continue to fry gently for a minute or two and then slowly add the milk. Turn up the heat and stir well until the sauce begins to boil. Reduce the heat and add the seasonings, herbs and cheese. Finally, add the lemon juice.

4 Fold the pancakes around 4 pieces of asparagus and pour the hot sauce over them. If necessary, microwave for a minute or so to heat through.

[recommended wines: Moulin Touchais Coteaux du Layon, Wittman Huxelrebe Spätlese, Vouvray Moelleux]

Sweet Onion Tartlets with Pecans and Roquefort

FOR THE PASTRY:
250 g. wholemeal flour
120 g. butter
1 tbsp. baking powder
salt
2 tbsps. sherry
water

FOR THE FILLING:
400 g. onions, thinly sliced (red onions, sweet onions or even spring onions)
30 g. butter
200 ml. single cream (or use sour cream)
2 eggs
100 g. Roquefort cheese
30 g. pecans

1 Fry the onions slowly in the butter to enhance their sweetness. You may choose to add a little sugar as they are frying.

2 Mix the flour and other ingredients for the pastry and slowly add the sherry and water to make a dough. Roll out and line individual quiches dishes.

3 Combine the eggs, cream and cheese and blend well.

4 Fill the pastry cases with the onions, sprinkle over the pecans and pour over the egg mixture.

5 Cook in a moderate oven at 180°C, 350°F, gas mark 4 for about 20 minutes until set and brown.

[recommended wines: Mariquita Californian White]

Raspberry Mousse

400 g. raspberries	2 tbsps. agar (or similar gelling agent)
50 ml. framboise	4 eggs, separated
50 g. sugar	1 tbsp. lemon juice

1 Warm the framboise and add the raspberries. Keep on a low heat until the raspberries soften. Add the sugar and allow to dissolve. Blend well and force through a fine sieve to extract the pips.

2 Blend in the agar, the egg yolks and the lemon juice. Allow this mixture to cool.

3 Beat the egg whites until they hold their form and gradually fold into the raspberry mixture.

4 Refrigerate for several hours or place in the freezer for an hour or so.

[recommended wine: Masi Recioto della Valpolicella]

Tira Mi Su

FOR THE BASE:	FOR THE TOPPING:
250 g. Amaretti Biscuits	250 ml. coffee
150 g. ground almonds	180 g. plain chocolate
100 ml. orange liqueur or amaretto	2 tsps. agar (optional)
FOR THE MIDDLE LAYER:	1-2 tbsps. rum (optional)
400-500 g. mascarpone	

1 Grind the amaretti biscuits with the ground almonds and add the liqueur.

2 Spread this mixture into a 27 cm. flan dish and spread the mascarpone on top. If you like you could mash the mascarpone with a little grated orange rind and some honey before spreading it over.

3 Melt the chocolate in the coffee (carefully in a saucepan, in a bowl over some boiling water or in a microwave). Add the rum, if used, and blend in the agar making sure that it is well mixed in. Pour this mixture on top of the mascarpone and place in a fridge for 2 hours or more to set.

[recommended wines: Essensia Orange Muscat, Brown Bros Orange Muscat and Flora]

Macadamia and Blueberry Tart

FOR THE PASTRY:
60 g. butter
120 g. wholemeal flour
2 tbsps. demerara sugar
grated rind of an orange
3 tbsps. orange juice

FOR THE FILLING:
2 eggs
250 ml. corn syrup (or honey)
30 g. melted butter
juice of an orange
100 g. plain macadamias
140 g. blueberries

1 Mix all of the ingredients for the pastry and roll out and line a 25 cm. pastry case. The pastry is quite fragile and is best rolled between two sheets of bakewell (heavy-duty greaseproof paper).

2 Bake the pastry case blind in a hot oven at 200°C, 400°F, gas mark 6 for 8-10 minutes. Use some bakewell and some old beans as for the pecan pie(page 74).

3 If you wish to, first cook the blueberries for a short while in a little port. Spread the blueberries and macadamias into the pastry case and mix the other ingredients in a blender and pour over. While cooking, the blueberries may explode, so you may want to prick them first.

4 Cook in a moderate oven at 180°C, 350°F, gas mark 4 for 30 minutes until the top of the tart is brown, bubbling and toffee-like.

[recommended wine: Elysium Black Muscat]

Chapter Seven

A Mediterranean Dinner Party
(mostly Italian)

There are many rich flavours in this meal which make it ideal to do, in its entirety, as a gourmet feast to convert any meat eater and because it is easy to find a lovely array of wines which will complement it well. Perhaps it is more realistic to select five or six of the savoury dishes choosing, for instance, between the salads, between the Greek Vegetables and the Pumpkin alla Siciliana and finally between the Pasta Rolls and the Risotto.

The Baby Carrots were inspired by a similar dish presented before me at 'Le Vieux Moulin' as mentioned in the introduction to Chapter Two. They are ideal to pass around with drinks as your guests arrive so provide some toothpicks to facilitate their serving. Other baby vegetables could be served in a similar way at the same time as the carrots, either in truffle oil or a with a different dressing.

You will have realised that I am very keen on a salad medley if you have read Chapter Two. The salad may be plated up and put on the table before the guests arrive so there is one less thing to think about. The salad will glamorise the dinner table when your guests enter the dining room and the crispness and sharpness of a salad is the ideal way to start the tastebuds off and to accompany a wine such as a Sauvignon Blanc. The Mushroom and Cheese Salad is, indeed, rich and might go better with a dry, fruity Riesling from South Australia. The Spinach and Wild Mushrooms would seem to be a dish best suited to the autumn but I have picked and marinated St Georges mushrooms which occur in April and May and even found, at the same time, blewits. They both work well. Of course, fine, fresh bay boletes or ceps could be sliced, raw, into the salad.

I have Phil's (of Chapter 5 fame) wife, Jane, to thank for introducing me to the delights of goose eggs and, when she delivered several to my door, I put them into a ramekin with slices of black truffles and my dinner party guests that evening were very impressed. My ambition is to go on a truffle hunt but, until that happens successfully, I shall have to content myself with buying them in supermarkets. In the absence of truffles, you could try some mixed vegetables, asparagus, artichoke or even some chopped coriander.

I had the privilege of being the guest chef at my neighbouring hotel "The Marygreen Manor" which has a colourful history over the last 500 years. It was an interesting task to cook all of the food in my kitchen and carry it into the busy kitchens of the Marygreen. Their experienced chefs made light of presenting the dishes beautifully for the sixty-five people who attended the meal and the manager, Paul Pearson, skilfully selected some wines from the hotel's winelist to enhance the food that we served. I remember that he was most impressed by the idea of tender Greek vegetables cooked in Chardonnay and he

Andreas in his everyday attire!
See him in his shop in St. Anns, Tottenham

chose a rich Macon Lugny to accompany it. Obviously, you will choose vegetables which are easily available and in season but the selection that I have suggested is a good mixture of colour, taste and texture. You should try hard to find the Gigantes beans especially because Andreas (see Chapter Twelve) tells me that they are "like the rhino horn". Colocassi is also a little unusual but it will be found in any good Cypriot food shop and it has a lovely texture. It should be well cooked (but not mushy) as it has a corrosive effect if eaten raw.

I invented the dish "Pumpkin alla Siciliana" many years ago and often mention its qualities. The pumpkin flesh is perfect to absorb the lovely flavours of the wine, marjoram and garlic. I have been running a campaign to promote the pumpkin, a sadly underrated vegetable in the U.K., and this dish should help me in this campaign.

The next two dishes are a little unusual and are bound to be a talking point at your dinner parties. The pasta roll seems a little involved but it always turns out so well that it is worth having a go to produce such an interesting presentation and flavour. Moreover, apart from the final warming in the melted butter with parmesan, it can be made well in advance and it could be served on a tomato sauce or a creamy herb sauce if you like. The wild wild risotto is another dish that has been in my repertoire for a while and the deep, chewy flavours are great with a Burgundy such as a Musigny or a Bonnes Mares, or, for a more available wine, try a Savigny-lès-Beaune.

The wine will be good, also, with the Oyster Mushrooms. These are always available in supermarkets and they go so well in a herby wine and tomato sauce. This dish would go well with some good quality pasta.

The Zuccotto is my trade mark dessert so, although it featured in *Vegetarian Dinner Parties*, it had to appear in this book, too. I take around 800 portions to the Fairport Cropredy Festival each year and the band and friends are always keen to finish off any leftovers at the late-night back-stage party.

I fell in love with the flavours and colours of the fruits in the Refreshing Fruit Salad while in Australia in 1998. Bern asked me not to tempt him with rich desserts so combinations of fruit were the best low calorie choice and I was most struck by the four fruits you will find in this recipe. Moreover, it is a most colourful selection to border the gâteau, although the wonderful presentation by the chef at the Marygreen Manor last year impressed all of the diners that evening. The pieces of gâteau were placed on a raspberry coulis with a mango coulis which were attractively interlaced. Whichever way it is served, the gâteau is bound to impress.

Some beautiful, fresh St. George's mushrooms (left), dried Shiitake (centre front), ordinary mushrooms (right) and Jew's Ears, together with jars of preserved Blewits and St. George's mushrooms

Baby Carrots in Truffle Oil

2 bunches baby carrots, washed
with most of the green leaves
removed

salt

pinch pepper
3 tbsps. truffle oil
deep-fried chervil or parsley

1 Boil or steam the carrots for 3 minutes and cool quickly.

2 Season and drizzle the oil over the carrots.

3 Garnish with the parsley or chervil. Serve, possibly with toothpicks, as an entrée.

Mushroom and Cheese Salad with a Brandy and Cream Dressing

400 g. button mushrooms, sliced
(bay boletes and ceps are
wonderful in this salad)

large bunch rocket

bunch basil

200 g. carrots, grated

200 g. celeriac, grated

100 g. parmesan (Reggiano), very
thinly sliced

80 g. large black olives

50 g. lightly toasted pumpkin seeds

FOR THE DRESSING:

2 tbsps. balsamic vinegar

2 tbsps. lemon juice

pinch pepper

salt

2 cloves garlic

half tsp. mustard

2 tbsps. double cream

2 egg yolks

80 ml. extra virgin olive oil

3 tbsps. brandy

1 Combine all of the ingredients for the salad or border the salad with the carrots and celeriac in separate rings (and, then, maybe, use some beetroot as well).

2 In a food processor, blend well the first 6 ingredients and slowly add the cream, egg yolks and olive oil, blending well at each stage. Finally, add the brandy (according to taste).

3 Mix the dressing into the salad just before serving.

Some of the olive bread (page 58) would be good to mop up the dressing.

Young Spinach Leaves with Marinated Wild Mushrooms and Pinenuts

FOR THE PRESERVED MUSHROOMS:

200 ml. vinegar (I usually use red wine vinegar)

400 ml. water

400 g. wild mushrooms , sliced (Bay boletes and ceps are best, blewits work alright)

salt

extra virgin olive oil to cover the mushrooms in a jar

FOR THE SALAD:

300 g. young spinach leaves (or a leaf mixture)

50 g. pinenuts, lightly toasted

1 Boil the vinegar with the water and salt and throw in the mushrooms.

2 After 5 minutes of boiling, extract the mushrooms carefully from the saucepan and place them on clean teatowels to drain and cool.

3 When the mushrooms are cool, spoon them into a very clean jar and top up with extra virgin olive oil.

4 Mix the mushrooms, spinach leaves and pinenuts with a little of the olive oil from the jar.

Truffle and Goose Egg Ramekins

3 black truffles, thinly sliced
2 goose eggs (or use 5 chicken eggs)
250 ml. double cream
salt

good pinch pepper
TO GARNISH:
green leaves (see below)

1 Grease 6 small ramekin dishes well with butter and place the truffles evenly at the base of each.

2 Mix the eggs with the cream and seasoning.

3 Place the ramekin dishes in a large flan dish and pour in a couple of centimetres of water.

4 Bake at 180°C, 350°F, gas mark 4 for about 25 minutes until set and just beginning to brown.

5 Turn out the ramekins onto small plates and garnish with green leaves e.g. wild garlic and chervil, or rocket and fennel.

Greek Vegetables in White Wine

50 ml. extra virgin olive oil

100 g. shallots, halved

4 artichoke hearts, quartered

300 g. colocassi, cubed (or use navets i.e. baby turnips, or Jerusalem artichokes or new potatoes)

250 g. gigantes beans, cooked until tender (or large butter beans)

2 medium carrots, thickly sliced

2 courgettes, thickly sliced

200 g. okra, topped and tailed (or use green beans)

100 g. oyster mushrooms (or any wild mushroom; "hen" of the woods is very good)

1 bottle Chardonnay (or any dry white wine)

salt

2 cloves garlic, finely chopped

1 tbsp. parsley and/or coriander

1 tbsp. fresh thyme

1 Cook the colocassi, artichokes and shallots briefly in the olive oil and add the Chardonnay and other ingredients.

2 Cook slowly for about an hour until all the vegetables are cooked but not soft. You may like to make this dish well in advance and reheat in a moderate oven.

3 When serving, make sure that each person has a good selection of the ingredients.

Pumpkin alla Siciliana

1 kg. pumpkin or butternut squash, cubed

100 ml. extra virgin olive oil

3 cloves garlic, crushed

2 tbsp. fresh marjoram (or 1 tbsp. dried)

400 ml. white wine (Soave works well)

salt

150 ml. double cream

1 Cook the pumpkin briefly in the oil and throw in the wine, salt, marjoram and garlic.

2 Simmer for about 20 minutes and strain off the surplus wine.

3 Pour in the cream and heat through without boiling.

Spinach (or Nettle) Pasta Rolls

FOR THE PASTA:
250 g. pasta flour (more if necessary)
3 eggs
salt
FOR THE FILLING:
40 g. pinenuts, gently toasted
400 g. cooked, chopped and drained spinach or nettles

250 g. ricotta
60 g. parmesan, finely grated
pinch grated nutmeg
salt
good pinch pepper
TO SERVE:
40 g. butter, melted
40 g. parmesan, finely grated

1 Mix the flour, eggs and salt in a food processor until the dough forms a ball. Wrap in clingfilm and allow to rest for 30 minutes or so.

2 Mix the ingredients for the filling.

3 Roll out the dough with a rolling pin until it is very thin and even.

4 Spread the filling over the dough leaving a 3 centimetre border all the way round.

5 Roll up the dough like a Swiss roll and secure the ends by pinching well.

6 Wrap the long cylinder in clean muslin and tuck any spare muslin under the roll.

7 Boil some water in a large saucepan and insert the roll. Simmer for about 20 mins.

8 Allow to cool in some cold water. Slice the roll into 3 centimetre pieces and place on an oven-proof dish. Sprinkle over the parmesan and melted butter and bake briefly for 10 minutes in a hot oven at 200°C, 400°F, gas mark 6.

Wild Wild Risotto

500 g. wild mushrooms (ceps or other boletes and honey fungus are good)

2 cloves garlic, crushed

300 g. basmati brown rice, cooked

300 g. wild rice, cooked

50 g. pinenuts

100 g. butter

50 ml. olive oil

1 tsp. tarragon, chopped

200 ml. double cream

1 tsp. mustard

salt

half tsp. black pepper

80 g. pecorino Romano, coarsely grated

1 In most of the butter and olive oil, fry the garlic and mushrooms until they soften. Slice some of the mushrooms but leave some whole.

2 In the remainder of the butter and oil, fry the pinenuts until golden.

3 Combine the rices and stir in the mushrooms, nuts, cream, mustard, tarragon and season with salt and freshly ground black pepper. Add some red wine to moisten if necessary.

4 Put into an ovenproof dish and cover. Cook in a moderate oven at 180°C, 350°F, gas mark 4 for 30 minutes.

5 Stir in the Pecorino and put back in the oven for a further 15 minutes or so.

Oyster Mushrooms Provençal

2 shallots, finely chopped

350 g. oyster mushrooms, sliced

400 g. tin tomatoes, puréed

150 ml. red wine

juice of 1 lemon

75 ml. olive oil

2 bayleaves

salt

good pinch pepper

1 Put all the ingredients in a saucepan and simmer for about 50 minutes until the mushrooms are soft and the sauce is well reduced. You could cook in a moderate oven for the same length of time. Serve warm.

Zuccotto

FOR THE SPONGE:
40 g. unsalted butter, melted
4 eggs, beaten
160 g. wholemeal flour
160 g. sugar
1 tsp. baking powder
amaretto to pour into the sponge
FOR THE FILLING:
60 g. dried apricots, slivered and soaked in muscat
60 g. dried mango, cut small and soaked in sambuca
60 g. dried bananas, finely chopped and soaked in banana liqueur

60 g. dried pineapple, cut small and soaked in Malibu
60 g. raisins, preferably lexias, soaked in rum
500 ml. double cream, whipped until firm (or use mascarpone)
60 g. roasted hazelnuts
60 g. flaked almonds
FOR THE TOPPING:
250 ml. double cream, whipped until thick
40 ml. carob syrup
40 ml. coffee or chocolate liqueur

1 Mix the sugar, baking powder and flour into the melted butter and slowly blend in the beaten eggs.

2 Bake in the centre of a moderate oven set at 180°C, 350°F, gas mark 4 for about 30 minutes until set and brown. If it browns before it is cooked through, you will have to cover the sponge. It is a good idea to bake the sponge on baking parchment so that you can simply peel it off when it cools down.

3 Ensure that the dried fruits are well soaked in the liqueurs by turning them from time to time. Mix them with the cream and nuts.

4 Line a hemispherical mixing bowl with a few strips of baking parchment and line it with thin fingers of sponge so that they completely line the bowl. Sprinkle with the amaretto.

5 Pile in the filling of cream, fruits and wine and top with more of the sponge. Place in the refrigerator overnight with a heavy plate on top.

6 Turn out the gâteau and cover with the mixture of cream, carob and coffee or chocolate liqueur.

The gâteau will keep well in the freezer until required and it is worth noting that a flat one is easier to cut and portion. Individual portions are also good to assemble and serve but you will need more topping. A slice of Zuccotto with some of the colourful fruit salad around the plate is a very attractive presentation.

Refreshing Fruit Salad

125 g. fresh raspberries
125 g. blueberries
3 kiwifruit, peeled and sliced

2 large oranges, peeled and sliced
30 ml. framboise

1 Layer the ingredients in an attractive fruit salad bowl and pour over the framboise. Refrigerate for several hours to allow the flavours to develop.

Zuccotto

Chapter Eight

Finger Food Party

The ideas of this chapter (and others from elsewhere in the book) may be used together to create an array of food which may be passed around at an informal gathering or they may be used as entrées to present to guests before the main dinner party commences. The size and number of different dishes for either purpose will depend on the numbers attending and the length of time that the event is to last with a further consideration if used as an entrée that they should whet the appetite and not depress it. A glass or several of Green Point Brut would go well with all of these offerings.

Goats Cheese Tartlets

FOR THE PASTRY:
250 g. wholemeal flour
120 g. butter
8 sun-dried tomatoes, soaked overnight
1 tbsp. baking powder
pinch salt
water

FOR THE FILLING:
6 basil leaves, slivered
200 ml. single cream
2 eggs
100 g. soft goat's cheese

1 Mix the flour and other ingredients for the pastry and slowly add the water to make a dough. Roll out and line mince pie tins.

2 Combine the eggs, cream and cheese and blend well.

3 Place a half a basil leaf in each tartlet and fill with the cheese mixture.

4 Cook in a moderate oven at 180 C, 350 F, gas mark 4 for about 20 minutes until set and brown.

Chanterelle Tartlets

FOR THE PASTRY: see above, but leave out the sun-dried tomatoes if you wish

FOR THE FILLING:
120 g. chanterelles, finely chopped
20 g. butter
1 tbsp. olive oil
1 shallot, finely chopped

1 tbsp. wholemeal flour
2 tbsps. milk
2 tbsps. white wine
salt
pinch black pepper
1 tsp. parsley, finely chopped

1 Roll out the pastry as above and cook the tartlet cases in a moderate oven at 180°C, 350°F, gas mark 4 for 12 minutes.

2 Fry the shallots in the oil and butter for a minute or two and throw in the chanterelles. Continue to fry for 3 minutes increasing the heat, if necessary, to expel some of the liquid from the mushrooms.

3 Add the flour and, stirring constantly, slowly pour in the milk and wine. After a couple of minutes the sauce should begin to thicken. Throw in the salt, pepper and parsley.

4 Spoon the mixture into the pastry cases and return to the oven for a further 5 minutes.

"Sausage" Rolls

FOR THE PASTRY: see above
FOR THE FILLING:
3 tbsps. sunflower oil
1 medium onion, finely chopped
half tbsp. dried basil

2 tbsps. tomato purée
250 g. puréed chestnuts
TO GLAZE:
1 egg, beaten

1 Heat the oil and fry the onion until transparent. Mix in the basil, tomato purée and chestnuts. Allow to cool.

2 Roll out the pastry into a rectangle about 10 centimetres by 30 centimetres. Put a 2-3 centimetre strip of the filling along the length of the pastry but 1-2 centimetres from the edge. Roll up the pastry and press down firmly to make a cylinder that is well sealed.

3 Tidy up the ends of the roll and brush with beaten egg. Cut into 6 "sausage" rolls before baking in a moderate oven at 180°C, 350°F, gas mark 4 for 20 minutes until golden brown.

Morel Tartlets

FOR THE PASTRY: see above
FOR THE FILLING:
25 g. butter
1 tbsp. olive oil
30 g. dried morels, soaked for several hours

1 shallot, finely chopped
15 strands good quality saffron
salt
pinch black pepper
100 ml. double cream

1 Make and cook the pastry as in the previous recipe.

2 Make sure the morels are well cleaned by putting them in a few changes of water if necessary.

3 Fry the morels and shallots in the oil and butter for 3 minutes until the shallots are softening

4 Add the other ingredients and cook on a very low heat for 10 minutes or so.

5 Spoon the mixture into the tartlet cases ensuring that each one contains a morel.

6 Put the tartlets back into the moderate oven for a further 5 minutes.

Pumpkin Balls

500 g. pumpkin, peeled and steamed until just cooked
180 g. feta
1 tbsp. coriander leaves, finely chopped

half tsp. sage, finely chopped
2 cloves garlic, finely chopped
salt
breadcrumbs and/or flour

1 Drain the pumpkin well.

2 Mash all the ingredients together and add sufficient flour and/or breadcrumbs to make a stiff mixture and place in the refrigerator for an hour or so.

3 Roll into walnut sized balls and fry in hot olive oil until golden.

4 Serve hot or cold.

Stuffed Mushrooms

12 closed cup mushrooms,
about 6 centimetres across

1 black truffle, finely sliced

30 g. butter

1 shallot, finely chopped

1 clove garlic, finely chopped

50 ml. dry white wine

50 ml. crème fraîche

1 egg yolk

60 g. breadcrumbs

good pinch black pepper

pinch nutmeg

salt

1 Wipe the mushrooms clean, take the stalk off each mushroom and carefully cut out as much of the gills as you can without breaking the mushroom.

2 Place a thin slice of truffle in each mushroom and set aside while you make the filling.

3 Fry the shallots and garlic in the butter for a few minutes until it softens. Add the white wine and throw in the chopped stalks and insides of mushrooms.

4 After 5 or 6 minutes stir in the rest of the ingredients and allow to cool slightly.

5 Press the filling firmly into each mushroom and bake in a moderate oven at 180°C, 350°F, gas mark 4 for 20 minutes until brown on top and the mushrooms themselves slightly shrivelled and beginning to soften.

Almond Aioli

4 cloves garlic

2 egg yolks

salt

300 ml. olive oil

3 tbsps. lemon juice

60 g. breadcrumbs

60 g. ground almonds

3 tbsps. parsley, finely chopped

pinch chilli powder

1 Blend the garlic and egg yolks together in the food processor and add the lemon juice and salt.

2 Slowly drizzle in the olive oil and, when thick, blend in the other ingredients.

3 Serve with the polenta and small, halved, hollowed out tomatoes.

Fried Polenta

150 g. polenta
salt
50 ml. olive oil
60 g. parmesan, finely grated

1 egg, beaten
fine breadcrumbs
olive oil for frying

1 Bring a half litre of water to the boil in a large saucepan.

2 Pour in the polenta in a slow stream, stirring constantly to avoid lumps. Use a long wooden spoon to stir the polenta as it will "spit" while it is being cooked.

3 Add the salt and the olive oil. Stir well and add the parmesan cheese.

4 Cook on a low heat for 20 minutes (or follow the instructions in the case of instant polenta) until the polenta is smooth and soft. When ready it should come away from the sides of the pan as you stir.

5 Pour the polenta into a greased tin and smooth into an even layer.

6 Allow the polenta to cool and set, a minimum of an hour.

7 Cut the set polenta into small 4 centimetre squares. Dip each square in beaten egg and coat well in breadcrumbs.

8 Fry in olive oil until golden brown all over. Drain on kitchen paper.

9 Serve with the tapenade and almond aioli.

Tapenade

200 g. black olives, pitted
100 g. Californian walnuts, lightly toasted
40 g. capers
2 cloves garlic

half tsp. tarragon
1 tsp. parsley
pepper or chilli to taste
brandy

1 In a food processor, blend all the ingredients and add sufficient brandy to make a stiff, spreading consistency. Serve with the polenta or spoon into halved cucumber with the pips removed.

Crocchette di Patate

900 g. potatoes, peeled and boiled in salted water

3 eggs

100 g. parmesan

handful parsley, finely chopped

half tsp. grated nutmeg

half tsp. pepper

salt

200 g. mozzarella, cut into 2 centimetre cubes

2 or 3 eggs, beaten

breadcrumbs

olive oil for frying

1 Drain the potatoes and mash them. Add the eggs, parmesan, parsley, nutmeg, pepper and a little salt. Mix well and leave to rest in a cool place for an hour or so.

2 Form the mixture into small rugby ball shape, about 6 centimetres long and 4 centimetres wide with a cube of mozzarella in the centre of each.

3 Roll each ball in the egg and breadcrumbs and fry in hot olive oil until golden brown.

"Chicken" or Cauliflower Bhajis

250 g. chicken of the woods or 6 cauliflower florets

FOR THE BATTER:

2 cloves garlic

small piece ginger

100 g. gram flour

1 tsp. cumin powder

1 tsp. coriander powder

half tsp. baking powder

salt

oil for frying

1 Blend all the ingredients for the batter and add enough water (or real ale) to make a thick batter.

2 If you are using the "chicken" or another mushroom, make sure it is clean and slice it thickly. If you are using cauliflower, steam for 3 minutes and drain well.

3 Coat the "chicken" or cauliflower florets in the batter and fry in hot oil until crisp and brown, about 5 minutes. Serve with cranberry sauce (see page 51).

Stuffed Artichoke Hearts

6 globe artichokes	2 tbsps. parsley, finely chopped
juice and rind of 2 lemons	2 tbsps. olive oil
40 g. breadcrumbs	salt
60 g. wild mushrooms	pinch black pepper
(ceps are the best)	6 slices Gruyère
2 cloves garlic, finely chopped	2 tbsps. olive oil

1 Heat the olive oil and fry the mushrooms with the garlic for 2 minutes.

2 Add in the parsley, breadcrumbs, salt, pepper and juice of 1 lemon. Set aside.

3 Cut off the stalks of the artichokes and remove about two rows of outer leaves of the artichokes. It is a good idea to wear rubber gloves to avoid staining of your hands.

4 Cut about 2 centimetres off the top of the artichokes and also any remaining sharp tips to any leaves. Rub each cut surface with lemon juice as you go.

5 Scoop out the hairy choke from the centre of each artichoke and brush the cut surface with lemon juice.

6 Put a portion of stuffing in each artichoke and steam for 40 minutes until just tender.

7 Place a slice of Gruyère on the stuffing of each artichoke heart and a little lemon rind.

8 Place under a hot grill for a couple of minutes until the cheese is melted and beginning to brown.

9 Serve cold or as a starter with tarragon sauce (see page 83).

Chapter Nine

A Vegetarian Barbecue/Picnic

have always enjoyed a vegetarian barbecue on a hot day but such occasions are rare in the U.K. Consequently, most of the practice for this chapter has been done in Balgowlah Heights, Sydney, the home of my dear friends, Bern and Julia. They have a powerful gas barbecue in their garden and it is ideal for cooking up some of the beautifully fresh vegetables which are on sale in their local shops. Served with a few dips, breads, salsas and salads, these marinated and barbecued vegetables are both healthy and tasty and are excellent with some of the powerful wines of the nearby Hunter Valley such as Chardonnays from Scarborough, Thalgara, Lakes Folly, Rosemount, Lindemans and Allandale along with some excellent reds like the stunning Peterson's Pinot Noir and smoky Shiraz from Rothbury and Brokenwood. When I arrived there for the first time in 1990 I knew nothing about Australian wines but Bernard has been a most helpful teacher on this subject. The only visit when my knowledge of vegetarian barbecues did not progress was 1994 when the nearby bushfires and the ensuing fire ban meant that even a safe barbecue was outlawed.

In the U.K., the few barbecues have entailed a gas bottle, a portable stove and a griddle pan. This arrangement can be swiftly set up in a country park, again to create wonderful outdoor eating. Barbecues eaten before watching the Blackmore Morris Men performances on a Wednesday evening were occasionally fraught when pub landlords realised that my idea of a vegetarian picnic and theirs were very different ("I thought you meant sandwiches!"). Walks to the Pontneddfechan Waterfall (mentioned in Chapter Twelve) have occasionally involved some cooking using the plentiful supplies of local firewood. The great advantage of such a location on a hot day is the provision of a cool place for the wine: i.e. the clear, fast flowing water of the nearby river.

Many other dishes in this book (as well as in *Vegetarian Dinner Parties*) would be great at a vegetarian barbecue and/or picnic. The 'Outdoor Meals' chapter of *Vegetarian Dinner Parties* deals well with the equipment that you should take on a picnic. For any outdoor event the main ingredient is good weather.

Barbecued Vegetables etc.

A SELECTION OF:

courgettes, green or yellow or both, sliced lengthways

pumpkin, sliced

pepper, quartered

small aubergines, halved

baby corn (ideally, still with leaves on)

mushrooms

baby onions

baby carrots

sweet or new potatoes, par cooked

halloumi cheese, sliced

tempeh, sliced

tofu, sliced

FOR THE MARINADE:

100 ml. extra virgin olive oil

salt

pepper

bunch basil or coriander

4 cloves garlic

AND, OPTIONALLY:

3 tbsps. white wine

3 tbsps. good soy sauce

3 tbsps. mirin

3 tbsps. Worcester sauce

3 tbsps. brandy

harissa

1 Mix up the ingredients for the marinade or make different marinades and use with different ingredients and a selection of herbs.

2 Put the vegetables and even the tofu, tempeh and halloumi into plastic containers with lids (or glass mixing bowls, cling-filmed), add the marinade(s) and leave for several hours, shaking from time to time so that the vegetables etc. are well coated.

3 Place the vegetables etc. on a hot barbecue and turn from time to time until tender and beginning to brown. Serve with a selection of breads and salsas/dips.

Lime and Coriander Dressing for the Halloumi

juice of 1 lime
2 tbsps. coriander leaves, finely chopped
1 tsp. whole-grain mustard

2 tbsps. balsamic vinegar
50 ml. extra virgin olive oil
salt
1 tbsp. capers

1 Blend all of the ingredients together and spoon over the barbecued (or fried) halloumi.

Avocado Salsa

2 medium, ripe avocados
2 tomatoes
juice of 1 lime
salt
2 tbsps. coriander leaves

half a red chilli (or more to taste)
1 small red onion (or use spring onions)
1-2 tbsps. olive oil

1 Put all of the ingredients on a large chopping board and chop until they are well mixed and smooth but still with some texture.

Red Macadamia Pesto

6 sun-dried tomatoes, soaked
overnight

bunch red basil (or use green)

100 g. macadamia nuts

2 cloves garlic

100 g. pecorino Romano, grated

50 ml. extra virgin olive oil

1 Put all of the ingredients in the food processor and blend until fairly smooth.

Smoked Tofu and Orange Salsa

220 g. smoked tofu

1 medium orange, peeled and
chopped

4 spring onions, very finely
chopped

1 tbsp. sherry vinegar

1 tbsp. sesame oil

1 tbsp. tamari soy sauce

TO GARNISH:

alfalfa sprouts

coriander leaves

1 Put all of the ingredients in a food processor and mix well.

2 Serve in a bowl bordered with alfalfa and with a few coriander leaves over the top.

Leon simultaneously practising his barbecue skills and dispensing some culinary advice in Bernard's garden

Chapter Ten

Festival Food

 start this chapter with a list of the festivals (could it be called a festivalography?) at which I have been present since my first one back in June 1980, together with any memories from them:

21&22 June, 1980. The Knebworth Festival (featuring Beach Boys and Santana).   At which £800 was lost.

6 July, 1980. The Milton Keynes Hot Air Balloon and Kite Festival
This festival was more a "spectacle" of Frisbee throwing.

26 July 1980. Milton Keynes Superbowl (featuring Police, UB40 and Squeeze)
"I think it's gonna rain today" reported the Melody Maker headline. After the rain but before we had sold anything, Bern advised me to emigrate. He now lives in Sydney; I am still in Brentwood.

14 &15 August, 1981. The Fairport Convention "Reunion" at Broughton Castle. This was the start of a beautiful relationship with the band and many of their associates. Thanks for everything, boys and Chris.

September 4-6, 1981. The Rougham Tree Fair.
These festivals are still remembered by many who grieve over their demise. I have heard it said that if you remember a Rougham then you were not there! I do, however, remember an American with a guitar who had no English money so, rather than take some dollars from him, he sang "Leon's Blue Cheese Quiche Blues" for his lunch.

June 5, 1982. The Strawberry Fair, Cambridge.

18-20 June, 1982. The Glastonbury CND Festival (featuring Van Morrison, U2 and many more).
The first Glastonbury was a wonderful event. It was both wet and dry (alternately) and I had the first semblance of a staff rebellion when Marianne was heard to mutter "Some of us are having to work unacceptably hard back here". A photograph of my stall eventually appeared in the book "Living in the Future" by Isaac Asimov with the caption "Vegetarianism is catching on in the affluent west for a number of reasons, not all of them connected with health."

13&14 August, 1982. The Fairport Convention "Reunion" at Cropredy
This was the first visit to a field that has become to feel like a second home. The Concert can now be re-lived on a wonderful video entitled "Forever Young".

3-5 September, 1982. The Rougham Tree Fair
As far as I can tell, this was the last one. As predicted in the Souvenir Programme: "Could this be the LAST Rougham Tree Fair. It may have become too big."
Sadly, yes.

More Vegetarian Dinner Parties

11 June 1983. The Strawberry Fair, Cambridge.

17-19 June, 1983. The Glastonbury CND Festival.
This was our first experience of queues at the stall (and I still have a treasured photograph to prove it! See page 114), so much so that our right hand neighbour was effectively "blocked out" by our queue on the Saturday and begged that it should stretch in the other direction on Sunday.

5-7 August, 1983. The Goodwood Folk Festival
This was another memorable event (or non-event for some). It was superbly organised with wonderful artistes and a fantastic concept of stages set up opposite the stands of the racecourse. However, it was not publicised so that even a pub a mile distant did not know of the festival's existence. I was the audience for a wonderful set by Peter Rowan! The Festival was declared bankrupt on the Sunday and artistes were paid a percentage of their agreed fee by a TV company who had planned a 6 programme series based on the music at the festival (but they used one crowd shot throughout, when they managed to collect together all traders, artistes and anyone else.)

12&13 August, 1983. The Fairport Convention "Reunion" at Cropredy.

19&20 August, 1983. The Northampton Tudor Rose Folk Festival
Hats off to T.W. who embezzled the rent so that when we arrived at the festival, we had to pay again. Still, the music was lovely (Home Service, Maddy Prior Band, Jim Couza, etc.)

26-29 August, 1983. The Lyng (nr. Norwich) Midsummer Dream Fair
The rent for this one was £8 per day...aaaah, those were the days. The top of the bill was Donovan (who had seemed out of sorts playing for whatever sum and in front of not many at Goodwood.) He was staggeringly good, but stage security was non-existent. Fortunately, my stall backed on to the stage and the great man had to borrow my stepladders to get up on to the stage where he was surrounded by 30 or so little children. My mother and I watched on, spellbound, from the back of the stage only panicking when asked if we knew how to mend his broken guitar string! As far as I can remember, a sneaky look at the organisers list revealed that Donovan was paid £2500. The next performer down, Bo The Clown, was on £40!

9-11 September, 1983. The Leeds Folk Festival.
It makes me shiver to look back through the programme and see who was appearing (and to see their photographs!). However, for me, this festival is remembered most for the destruction of my wooden frame stall in a windy squall. The structure landed on my mother and, I am glad to say, she recovered; the stall never did.

2 June, 1984. The Strawberry Fair, Cambridge

22-24 June 1984. The Glastonbury CND Festival (featuring Fairport Convention)

10-11 August, 1984. The Fairport Convention "Reunion " at Cropredy

8 September, 1984. The Peckham Rye Festival
This one featured "Frankie goes to Peckham".

25 May, 1985. The Strawberry Fair, Cambridge.

21-23 June, 1985. The Glastonbury CND Festival (featuring Midnight Oil, The Pogues, etc.)
This was the first really wet one with a sea of mud invading the stall as Carolyn slept on in her camp bed. She was in danger of floating away when we rallied around (in spite of only one pair of wellies between us) and, after my father had made a make-shift rake with some waste wood, we managed to bale out and push the mud for to swamp the next stall down the hill.

7 July, 1985. Jobs For a Change Festival in Battersea Park.

4 August, 1985. Basildon Peace Fair.

9&10 August, 1985. Fairport Convention "Reunion" at Cropredy

7 June 1986. Strawberry Fair, Cambridge

20-22 June, 1986. The Glastonbury CND Festival (featuring Simply Red, Christy Moore etc.)
This was another sell-out year for us so I took the time to take a helicopter ride over the site...what a sight.

13 July, 1986. Basildon Peace Fair.

8&9 August, 1986. The Fairport Convention "Reunion" at Cropredy

22-25 August, 1986. The Preseli Folk Festival
In fact, we were so washed out and fed up that we left on the Sunday! Why is the August Bank Holiday weekend so miserable so often?

6 June, 1987. The Strawberry Fair, Cambridge.

19-21 June, 1987. The Glastonbury Festival
This was another particularly wet one but, somehow, we survived.

26 July - 1 August, 1987. The Israeli Folk Dance Association Summer Camp.
I was never asked to do this one again, zut alors. They said that my food made them fart while they were dancing! The revelation of this fact (off air) later had a giggly effect on Barbara Sturgeon on BBC Radio Kent, so much so that when we were back on air, I had to do all the talking for the first minute.

14&15 August, 1987. The Fairport Convention "Reunion" at Cropredy
This was a record breaker: we had a queue that disappeared, snakelike, past the adjacent stall.

21-23 August, 1987. Nostell Priory Rock Festival (featuring Jethro Tull)

28-31 August, 1987. Geldeston Hall Festival
This one was yet another stallholders' convention due to lack of publicity and any substantial entertainment (another wasted August Bank Holiday).

111

4 June, 1988. The Strawberry Fair, Cambridge

11 June, 1988. The Turnham Green Fair.

12 June, 1988. The Greenwich Against the Poll Tax Festival (featuring Squeeze)

22-24 July, 1988. The Village Pump Festival, Trowbridge (featuring Richard Thompson and many wonderful bands)
It was a great shame to be involved with such a pleasurable festival for only two years.

6&7 August, 1988. The Armada Pageant

12&13 August, 1988. The Fairport Convention "Reunion" at Cropredy

19-22 August, 1988. The First Lancaster Folk Festival (and, probably, the last)
This one was made memorable at the last by my favourite band throwing copies of my cookery book into the crowd. I hope they went to happy homes.

26-29 August, 1988. The Peterborough Country Music Festival
Just in case I needed any persuasion, this festival put me off country music for life, but the adjacent beer festival with the delights of an oompah band was adequate compensation.

Jules serving the queue at Cropredy

29 May, 1989. The Kingston Green Fair.
For some reason, just Helen and I tried to keep the eager queues at bay through an unexpectedly busy day. After that, Helen took everything in her stride. It was her first festival.

3 June, 1989. Strawberry Fair, Cambridge
I should say a little about the lovely Saturdays spent in early June each year on Midsummer Common. The early Fairs featured local talent and were very much "green" fairs with a sound ecological base and a wonderful array of stalls which attracted a diverse mix of people, mainly from the city of Cambridge. The food stalls were also varied but were, again, interesting and tending toward wholefood and vegetarian. Soon after the turn of the decade, there was a gradual change of direction so that in 1982 we paid £12 rent and in 1997, £566. This increase was to finance so-called "name" bands from outside the area which, in turn has led to a change in the type of people attracted to the Fair, which, nevertheless, still has many good points. I explain this ambivalence to my fans in Cambridge who have enjoyed my food at so many Fairs to account for my non-appearance now each June.

16-18 June, 1989. The Glastonbury Festival (featuring Elvis Costello, Flaco Jimenez, etc.)

The first appearance of the police at Glastonbury was welcomed by me and so was the wonderful atmosphere at this early Glastonbury at which takings nudged over £8000 (and costs nudged around £5000!)

14-16 July, 1989. The Village Pump Festival, Trowbridge (more fantastic music)

To coincide with Bastille Day number 200, we provided Feuilles de Vignes Farcies au Pâté de Noix Périgourdine, Ramequins de Champignons Sauvages Sauce Saffran, Gratin Savoyard and Ratatouille but suffered tradewise because no one could pronounce the dishes on the menu. Hearing Kathryn Tickell for the first time was a reasonable compensation. I heard that at the festival in 1990 at which I was not present, there was a "lament for Leon". The organisers obviously did not hear it.

22-23 July, 1989. The Lambeth Country Show.

28-30 July, 1989. The Treworgey Tree Fayre

The amazing publicity generated for this event ensured that "THE PEACE AND TRANQUILLITY OF A SCENIC WOODED VALLEY ON THE EDGE OF BODMIN MOOR WILL BE TOTALLY RUINED BY 3 DAYS OF LOUD MUSIC, HUNDREDS OF STALLS AND THOUSANDS OF PEOPLE". These were the words (and spelling) from the poster. The problem was that basic facilities such as security, water and toilets were sadly missing although the "Pleasure Dome" seemed, somehow, to function. In case you are curious, it was a huge, warm, communal shower area and a welcome relief from the rest of the festival. What happened to the portable toilets, you may ask. The suggestion is that they became stuck under a railway bridge, turned around and went home. A lesson to us all. Perhaps the organisers of Goodwood and Treworgey should get together. Nice try, K.D. Crabb, Esq.

18&19 August, 1989. The Fairport Convention "Reunion" at Cropredy

19 May, 1990. The Camden Spring Fair.

28 May, 1990. The Kingston Green Fair

2 June, 1990. The Strawberry Fair, Cambridge

22-24 June, 1990. The Glastonbury Festival of Contemporary Performing Arts

The essential guide to the festival i.e. the programme (price £3) gives some most important advice:- "If your specs are loose, don't peer down the bogs". This was the year when we were on a slope from left to right and, consequently, I finished the festival with one leg longer than the other.

Leon serves another customer at Cropredy while the next one ponders his choices.

28 July, 1990. Strawberry Fair, West Midlands

4&5 August, 1990. The Dudley Show

7-11, August. 1990. The Great British Beer Festival, Brighton Metropole
This was a most enjoyable, never-to-be-repeated, experience. We provided wall-to-wall curries and, in between, sampled some of the best beers, ciders and perries that Britain has to offer. Would that I could do more festivals where I could set up my stall and have no fear of rain or wind. This was because we set up inside the gigantic conference centre at the Metropole (and did a good job, I believe).

17&18 August, 1990. Fairport Convention at The Cropredy Festival

The never-ending queue at Glastonbury in 1983.   (Notice the chef's perks ↗)

27 May, 1991. The Kingston Green Fair

1 June, 1991. The Strawberry Fair, Cambridge

9 June, 1991. The Essex History Fair, Maldon

14 July, 1991. Southwark Irish Festival

19-21 July, 1991. WOMAD (World of Music and Dance) Festival, Reading
The start of a great association with a very well run festival that has fostered the support of local people and yet has provided entertainment from all around the world. The festival improves each year.

27 July, 1991. The Deptford Urban Festival

28 July, 1991. Vegetarian Picnic at Alexander Palace

30 July-4 August, 1991. The Gosport Festival.
No trade, but lots of lovely music and great company, this was a bit like a week long holiday on the South coast.

16&17 August, 1991. Fairport Convention at The Cropredy Festival

6 June, 1992. The Strawberry Fair, Cambridge

26-28 June, 1992. The Glastonbury Festival of Contemporary Performing Arts

17-19 July, 1992. WOMAD Festival, Reading

1 August, 1992. The Deptford Urban Festival

14&15 August, 1992. Fairport Convention at The Cropredy Festival

31 May, 1993. The Kingston Green Fair

13 June, 1993. The Essex History Fair, Waltham Abbey

25-27 June, 1993. The Glastonbury Festival of Contemporary Performing Arts
This was a great Glastonbury; which began inauspiciously when I opened the back of the van on arrival at the site only to find that my father had perched a large dustbin of marinated carrots on another dustbin in a highly unstable way. Much swearing ensued my partial drowning in garlic, vinegar and olive oil and the market managers were good enough to offer me a shower..in fact, they insisted on it! By the Sunday the smell had worn off. My father had trouble counting the money, so well did we do (so he was forgiven). Vicky's New Zealand humour and enthusiasm, Sue's organisational skills available once more after a few years off, Helen's experience, Lena's steadiness and Chloe on the food processor combined to make it the most successful festival yet and we still had time for some interesting visits to other stalls!

16-18 July, 1993. WOMAD Festival, Reading

7&8 August, 1993 The Bristol Community Festival (Ashton Court)

13&14 August, 1993. Fairport Convention at The Cropredy Festival
The Friday night was enlivened by the idiosyncratic band, The Leningrad Cowboys. It was great entertainment.

26-30 August,1993. The Chelmsford Spectacular.

May 30, 1994. The Kingston Kids Fair

4 June, 1994. The Strawberry Fair, Cambridge

11&12 June, 1994. The Colchester History Fair

24-26 June, 1994. The Glastonbury Festival of Contemporary Performing Arts
I even had time off from the stall to watch a marvellous concert by Mary Black.

22-24 July, 1994. WOMAD Festival, Reading

26-31 July 1994. The Big Green Gathering, Vale of the White Horse
Except that it was not so big, just very friendly.

12-13 August, 1994. Fairport Convention at The Cropredy Festival
A lovely man told me that he had been coming to the festival for many years with his friend who had passed away in the year just gone; his friend told him that he came to the festival as much to eat my food as to listen to the music.

26-29 August, 1994. WOMAD Festival, Morecambe
We were once more blessed with the luck of the late August Bank Holiday and were washed and blown away, simultaneously.

10 June, 1995. The Strawberry Fair, Cambridge

23-25 June, 1995. The Glastonbury Festival of Contemporary Performing Arts
In fact, by now, the festival had become a week long endurance test, with trading from Wednesday through to Monday.

15&16 July, 1995. The Bristol Community Festival (Ashton Court)

21-23 July, 1995. WOMAD Festival, Reading
It was at this festival that I was told by a man that he had enjoyed my food so much over the years that he had named his son after me.

29 July, 1995. The Deptford Urban Festival

11&12 August, 1995. Fairport Convention at The Cropredy Festival
I well remember the female members of my team extracting free t-shirts from the neighbouring stall by agreeing to wear them (and not much else, above the waist), wet. I have the photograph to prove it.

28 August, 1995. The Sutton Environmental Fair

24-26 May, 1996. The Bristol Festival of the Sea
The wind blew, the stall swayed and a table collapsed. Chinese vegetable curry all over the ground sheet was soon cleared up thanks to Gerry, Vannessa and Linda but we never recovered from the early morning flit from one pitch to another and then another at 6.30 p.m. on the Saturday and, by the end, I felt like walking the plank as long as some of the organisers preceded me. We did meet some charming old sailors (much to the girls' delight) and Paul McGann.

8 June, 1996. The Strawberry Fair, Cambridge

13&14 July, 1996. The Bristol Community Festival (Ashton Court)

19-21 July, 1996. The WOMAD Festival, Reading

27 July, 1996. The Folkestone Ecofair

9&10 August, 1996. Fairport Convention at The Cropredy Festival

17&18 August, 1996. V96 at Chelmsford

23-26 August, 1996. The Ashford Eurofest
...and beer festival. This was fortunate as, once again, we were in danger of sinking in the mud at the end of August. Why, why did they site the festival on the flood plain of the river?

27-29 June, 1997. The Glastonbury Festival of Contemporary Performing Arts
This was a tragic festival, so wet that moving around the festival was impossible. The van was pulled out by two tractors double-heading.

6 July, 1997. The Hook Norton Country Fair

19&20 July,1997. The Bristol Community Festival (Ashton Court)

25-27 July, 1997. The WOMAD Festival, Reading

8&9 August, 1997. Fairport Convention at The Cropredy Festival
The first attempt at providing a Lebanese Feast was so successful that we ran out of food at 7 p.m. with 15 people unsuccessfully queuing for a plateful.

16&17 August, 1997. V97 at Chelmsford

I am sure there will be many more festivals in the future and many more tales to tell. I have had to be innovative in my choice of dishes at festivals given the difficult conditions for producing gourmet vegetarian food. Hiring a walk-in coolroom has become essential at longer festivals and we have a range of different size vans hired from Budget to fulfil our different needs. How we used to cope with no refrigeration and, sometimes, just an estate car with the stall strapped to a roof rack, I do not know. For a couple of years I had a trailer, until it turned my car over on the M25 – yet another horror story. The greatest worry when planning a summer of outdoor catering is always the weather, but it always averages out and it does make life interesting.

The recipes given here reflect most of the dishes that I have served on my stall through the 18 years although you will find common favourites such as Tabbouleh; Celery, Stilton, Walnut and Port Quiche; and Herb and Cashew Nutroast with a Mango Stuffing elsewhere in the book. Add in the curries of Chapter Eleven and expect to find Chapter One on offer more and more . . . and pray for hot weather!

Greek Vegetable Stew

60 ml. olive oil

1 medium onion, finely chopped

60 g. bulgar

200 ml. (or more) dry white wine

100 g. carrots, chopped and par-boiled

200 g. spinach, finely chopped (I usually use tinned)

100 g. courgettes, chopped

200 g. tin tomatoes, puréed (or use 50 g. tomato purée)

2 cloves garlic, finely chopped

1 tsp. cumin

salt

1 tbsp. fresh coriander, finely chopped (or use coriander concentrate or dried coriander)

half tsp. chilli powder (to taste)

100 g. cooked cannelini beans (or blackeye beans)

60 ml. bitter orange juice

1 Fry the onion in the olive oil until transparent.

2 Stir in the bulgar and fry for a minute or two (Andreas throws in some vermicelli, too, here).

3 Add enough wine to cover and top up as necessary with more wine or the water in which the carrots were cooked.

4 Add the carrots, courgettes and spinach and the tomatoes.

5 Add the finely chopped garlic and the other seasonings.

6 Add the cooked cannelini beans or use tinned ones.

7 Finally, mix in the orange juice. Andreas describes the desired consistency as "medium thickness".

Lakhsa

1 tin coconut cream

1 tsp. lemon grass, chopped

750 ml. water

250 g. tofu, cubed

2 large broccoli florets, cut small

200 g. noodles

2 red chillis

small piece galangal or ginger

6 shiitake mushrooms, soaked and slivered

3 tbsps. soy sauce

1 Put all of the ingredients in a large saucepan and simmer for 30 minutes until the noodles are cooked. Other vegetables may be added to this recipe.

Butter Bean and Chilli Pie

FOR THE PASTRY:
400 g. wholemeal flour
100 ml. vegetable oil
salt
1 tbsp. baking powder
water

FOR THE FILLING:
3 tbsps. olive oil
1 large onion, finely chopped
3 cloves garlic, finely chopped
200 g. tomato purée
1 tbsp. dried basil
1 tbsp. chilli powder
(more or less, to taste)
500 g. butter beans,
cooked until soft

1 Combine the ingredients for the pastry and roll out a 20 centimetre pastry case.

2 Meanwhile, fry the onion and garlic in the olive oil until transparent and add the other ingredients.

3 Fill the pie and place a pastry lid on top. Seal well and bake at 180°C, 350°F, gas mark 4 for 30 minutes until brown.

Mediterranean Lentil Pie

FOR THE PASTRY:
see above (add some tomato purée
into the pastry if you wish)

FOR THE FILLING:
500 g. ratatouille, as in Chapter 2,
with or without pumpkin
500 g. cooked red or green lentils,
well drained

1 Mix the ratatouille with the dry lentils, fill the pie and cook as in the above recipe.

Spinach Pie with Feta Cheese and Pinenuts

FOR THE PASTRY: see above or use some butter or olive oil and an egg instead of the vegetable oil or use filo pastry

FOR THE FILLING:
800 g. tin spinach, well drained (or use nettles or a mixture of nettles and wild garlic, cooked)

100 g. feta cheese, cubed

100 g. pinenuts
1 medium onion, finely chopped
1 clove garlic, finely chopped
2 tbsps. olive oil
1 tsp. dried oregano
pinch nutmeg
FOR THE GLAZE:
beaten egg
1 tbsp. sesame seeds

1 Fry the onion and garlic in the olive oil until transparent and mix with the other ingredients for the filling.

2 Fill the pie as above and glaze with beaten egg. Sprinkle sesame seeds over the top of the pie and cook as above.

Curried Lentil Pie

FOR THE PASTRY: see above
FOR THE FILLING:
3 tbsp. vegetable oil
1 medium onion, finely chopped
1 clove garlic, finely chopped
1 small piece ginger, grated

1 tsp. ground cumin
1 tsp. ground coriander
1 tsp. turmeric
salt
500 g. cooked red lentils, puréed until smooth

1 Fry the onion and garlic in the oil until transparent and add the ginger and spices. Cook for a few minutes on a gentle heat and stir in the lentils.

2 Fill and cook the pie as above.

Russian Pie

FOR THE PASTRY: see above or
use some butter instead of the oil

FOR THE FILLING:
150 g. TVP (soya) chunks,
rehydrated in white wine
60 g. butter
1 medium onion, finely chopped

2 cloves garlic, finely chopped
200 g. button mushrooms
200 ml. sour cream
salt
good pinch pepper
1 tsp. mustard

1 Strain off the liquid from the TVP and reserve it.

2 Fry the onion and garlic in the butter for a few minutes.

3 Add the TVP and mushrooms. Stir and continue to cook over a medium heat for 5 minutes or so.

4 Add the sour cream, salt, freshly ground black pepper and mustard.

5 Simmer gently until the TVP is tender. Add the strained liquid if necessary.

6 Fill the pie and cook as in the above recipes.

Cheesy Vegetable Pie

FOR THE PASTRY: see above,
use butter if preferred

FOR THE FILLING:
500 g. vegetables, cooked (broccoli,
cauliflower, carrots, leeks, butter
beans, green beans, sweetcorn,
courgettes, etc.)
50 g. butter

1 small onion, finely chopped
50 g. wholemeal flour
250 ml. milk (and/or stock or
white wine)
200 g. strong cheddar, grated
salt
good pinch pepper

1 Melt the butter and fry the onion for a short while and throw in the flour. Cook briefly without browning and slowly add the milk, stirring constantly.

2 Bring the sauce to the boil and then simmer for 10 minutes or so and stir in the cheese and season.

3 Allow the sauce to cool before adding the vegetables.

4 Fill the pie and cook as for the above recipes. An egg glaze is good here.

Mixed Vegetable and Red Leicester Cheese Quiche With Herbs from my Garden

FOR THE PASTRY:
200 g. wholemeal flour
100 g. butter
1 tbsp. baking powder
salt
water

FOR THE FILLING:
200 g. mixed vegetables (frozen, found in all supermarkets, containing peas, carrots, sweetcorn, peppers, broccoli, etc.)

good handful mixed fresh herbs
100 g. Red Leicester Cheese
3 eggs
250 ml. single cream (or 50-50 milk and double cream)

1 Blend the flour with the butter, baking powder and salt. Add the water slowly to make a short crust pastry dough.

2 Roll out the pastry and line a 20 centimetre flan dish.

3 Place the vegetables evenly over the pastry case and sprinkle over the mixed herbs.

4 Combine the cheese, eggs and cream and pour it over the mixed vegetables.

5 Bake at 180°C, 350°F, gas mark 4 for 25 minutes until brown and set.

Three wonderful quiches

Quiche Niçoise

FOR THE PASTRY: see above
FOR THE FILLING:
2 tbsps. olive oil
1 medium onion, finely chopped
1 clove garlic, finely chopped
half tsp. dried oregano
half tsp. dried basil

400 g. tin tomatoes
125 g. blue cheese (Bleu d'Auvergne and Danish Blue are my favourites)
3 eggs
TO PUT ON TOP:
6 black olives
2 tbsps. parmesan, finely grated

1 Make the pastry as above.

2 Fry the onion and garlic in the olive oil until transparent and stir in the herbs.

3 Add the tinned tomatoes and cook for a further 15 minutes or so. Add a little tomato purée if you wish for a deeper red colour for your quiche.

4 Blend the cheese with the eggs and add the tomato mixture. Blend until well mixed but not smooth.

5 Fill the pastry case with this mixture and place the olives over the top in a circle. Sprinkle with the parmesan cheese.

6 Cook, as above, for 25 minutes.

Broccoli and Roquefort Quiche

FOR THE PASTRY: see above
FOR THE FILLING:
200 g. broccoli florets, cooked and chopped coarsely
50 g. flaked almonds

100 g. Roquefort cheese
3 eggs
250 ml. single cream (or 50-50 milk and double cream)

1 Make the pastry as above.

2 Place the broccoli on the pastry case and sprinkle over the almonds.

3 Blend the cheese, eggs and cream until smooth and pour over the broccoli.

4 Cook the quiche as above.

123

Flageolet and Sage Quiche

FOR THE PASTRY: see above
FOR THE FILLING:
200 g. flageolet beans, cooked until tender

120 g. sage Derby cheese
3 eggs
250 ml. single cream (or 50-50 double cream and milk)

1 Make the pastry as above.

2 Place the flageolets evenly over the pastry case.

3 Mix the cheese, eggs and cream and blend well.

4 Pour the mixture over the beans and cook as above.

Brazil Nut Roast

200 g. brazil nuts, ground
200 g. breadcrumbs, ground
2 tbsps. vegetable oil
1 medium onion, finely chopped
1 clove garlic, finely chopped
1 medium carrot, shredded
2 sticks celery, finely chopped

100 g. mushrooms, finely chopped
1 tbsp. tomato purée
1 tbsp. dried mixed herbs
1 tbsp. Miso (or use yeast extract)
100 ml. soya milk
stock or white wine if necessary

1 Fry the onion and garlic in the oil and add the carrot, celery, mushrooms and tomato purée. Fry for a few minutes

2 Add the herbs, miso and soya milk and cook for a few minutes further.

3 Mix all the ingredients together and add sufficient wine or stock to make a reasonably moist but firm mixture.

4 Fill a rectangular baking tin and bake in a moderate oven at 180°C, 350°F, gas mark 4 for 40 minutes, covered, and for 20 minutes uncovered. Alternatively, microwave for 15-20 minutes.

Mushroom and Cashew Nutroast

2 tbsps. vegetable oil
1 medium onion, finely chopped
200 g. mushrooms, finely sliced
250 g. cashews, ground
250 g. breadcrumbs, ground
200 ml. vegetable stock and/or
red wine

100 ml. soya milk
salt
pinch pepper
half tsp. dried mixed herbs
1 tsp. miso or soya sauce
3 whole flat mushrooms

1 Fry the onion until tender. Throw in the mushrooms and continue to fry for several minutes.

2 Mix the cashews, breadcrumbs and seasonings with the onion and stock or red wine and soya milk to give a moist but stiff consistency.

3 Lay whole mushrooms in an ovenproof dish. Fill with the cashew mix.

4 Bake in a moderate oven at 180°C, 350°F, gas mark 4 for an hour until brown or microwave for 15-20 minutes.

Wild Rice Salad

100 g. wild rice, cooked
200 g. short grain brown rice (or Basmati brown rice), cooked
1 red pepper, finely chopped
100 g. sweetcorn
100 g. petit pois

50 g. whole cashews
50 g. macadamias (or roasted hazels)
1 tsp. harissa
3 tbsps. sesame oil

1 Mix all the ingredients together and serve, possibly garnished with orange twists or slivered dried apricots.

(Chinese vegetables may be added into this salad)

New Potato Salad with a Smoked Tofu Mayonnaise

250 g. new potatoes, scrubbed and cooked until tender

100 g. walnuts

2 sticks celery, finely chopped

60 g. sunflower seeds, toasted in a little sunflower oil and soya sauce in the oven, under a grill (care!), in the microwave or in the frying pan

60 g. dried apricots, slivered

FOR THE MAYONNAISE:

50 g. soya flour

1 clove garlic

salt

pinch pepper

quarter tsp. mustard

1 tsp. sugar

50 ml. red wine vinegar

good tsp. miso

100 g. smoked tofu

50 ml. sunflower oil

200 ml. soya milk

1 Mix the ingredients together for the salad.

2 Blend the first 6 ingredients for the mayonnaise and blend in the vinegar, miso and tofu.

3 Pour in the oil and slowly add the soya milk to make a mayonnaise-like consistency.

4 Mix in with the salad and garnish, if you wish, with some chopped chives.

Marinated Carrots

500 g. carrots, cut into small cubes

60 ml. olive oil

60 ml. red wine vinegar

1 tbsp. dried oregano

salt

4 cloves garlic, finely sliced

1 Put all of the ingredients into a saucepan and cook fast for about 12 minutes so that the carrots are still quite firm.

2 Cool and serve or keep for up to 2 weeks in the refrigerator or longer if frozen. Combine with some chilli pickle to make a great curry accompaniment.

Pasta Salad

500 g. pasta spirals
200 g. mange touts, cooked and halved
200 g. baby corn, chopped
200 g. cherry tomatoes

few basil leaves
pinch pepper
3 tbsps. extra virgin olive oil
few pinenuts

1 Mix all the ingredients together and sprinkle with the pinenuts.

Caponata

60 ml. extra virgin olive oil
1 large aubergine, cubed
3 sticks celery, finely chopped (or use fennel)
2 tbsps. capers
2 tbsps. green olives

2 tbsps. sultanas (or currants)
1 tbsp. sugar
400 g. tin tomatoes
salt
50 ml. red wine vinegar

1 Put all of the ingredients in a saucepan and cook for 15 minutes or so until the aubergines are cooked.

2 Serve cold.

The potato salad

Carrot and Banana Salad

250 g. carrots, grated
60 g. sultanas, soaked in
lemon juice

2 bananas, sliced
60 g. flaked almonds

1 Mix all of the ingredients together and garnish, if you wish, with parsley.

Mexican Salad

200 g. green lentils, cooked
2 avocados, thinly sliced
2 medium oranges, peeled and
thinly sliced

1 red onion, thinly sliced
a few black olives
a few Californian walnuts
1 red chilli, finely chopped

1 Mix all of the ingredients together and serve with a few coriander leaves to garnish.

The stall at WOMAD in 1991

A typical "Leon plateful" which can keep most festival-goers satisfied for a long time

The field at Cropredy before the invasion . . .

. . . and after

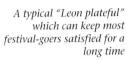

Helen's cake to celebrate the 25th Anniversary of Fairport Convention

Multi-coloured Coleslaw with Home-made Mayonnaise

250 g. Dutch white cabbage, shredded

250 g. red cabbage, shredded

250 g. carrots, grated

4 sticks celery, thinly sliced

200 g. toasted peanuts

few caraway seeds

FOR THE MAYONNAISE:

2 eggs

1 tsp. mustard

1 tsp. demerara sugar

salt

good pinch pepper

2 cloves garlic

50 ml. red wine vinegar

500 ml. sunflower oil

1 To make the mayonnaise, put all the ingredients except the oil into a food processor and blend well.

2 Slowly add the oil and wait until the tone changes. It is then ready to mix well into the mixture of vegetables and peanuts which have been lightly oiled and toasted until just browning.

Variations on the mayonnaise include adding herbs or watercress, tomato purée or harissa or adding more or less garlic and, perhaps, some olive oil for a heavier mayonnaise.

Noodle Salad

250 g. egg noodles, cooked for 4 minutes and drained

50 g. arame seaweed, soaked for an hour

2 tbsps. soy sauce

200 g. tofu, cubed

2 carrots, thinly sliced

2 peppers (different colours), sliced

50 g. sesame seeds

2 tbsps. sesame oil

100 g. sugar snap peas, cooked for 4 minutes

1 Mix all of the ingredients together.

Chapter Eleven

A Curry Party

F riends who know me well and the many hundreds of people who have attended my Indian Cookery Demonstrations will know my enthusiasm for cooking Indian food. Indeed, it was the first cookery skill that I mastered back at Emmanuel College in the dim and distant past. I regularly escaped the heady academia of the University to wander down Mill Road to collect inspiration and facts from a small Indian grocers and, given very limited cooking facilities in college rooms, I was able to experiment with different spicy recipes and, eventually, invite friends to my room to show off my newly learned skills. When I met up with Peter and the post-grad set at Little Shelford, I was able to expand my repertoire quickly, given a much larger kitchen and many more willing tastebuds. Over the years I have been brave enough to demonstrate my Indian recipe ideas in some most unlikely places such as Leicester and Bradford. I well remember the day when BBC Radio Leicester sent me to the home of an Indian family to cook them a curry. I was received most politely, if with some scepticism. The entertainment value of the exercise was high and I did partially win them over. Most of all, I received some practical hints which I still use to this day. At Rochester, I was told by an Indian lady that I cooked just like an Indian and in Bradford the only complaint was concerning my pronunciation of Indian words like 'Basmati'. Perhaps these compliments were eclipsed when I cooked a West Indian buffet in Tooting and was asked at the end "Are you West Indian, then?"

Nowadays, I find cooking curries such an easy operation even in a strange kitchen. Once you have all the basic ingredients in front of you, it is a quick process to create curries new and old and then to keep them warm for serving later by putting them in a low oven. Very little washing up is required if you recycle the saucepans and most of the cooking can be done well before the dinner party is to commence. Only the frying of the onion bhajis and samosas needs to be done at the last minute.

It may also be asked why I have relegated Indian food to the place of the penultimate chapter of the follow-up to *Vegetarian Dinner Parties* where it had prime position. It is mainly to be adjacent to the festival food chapter as, on many occasions, I have made huge quantities of curries at the festivals. This also accounts for the 'instant' nature of

131

some of the dishes in the chapter. A veritable dustbin of curry can be made in a matter of minutes with a tub of Chinese curry paste, a few large tins of Chinese vegetables and coconut cream, a few handfuls of cashews and some frozen vegetables. It is quite

Beer and Onion Bhajis (see page 134) with a good selection of pickles

embarrassing, in view of the simplicity of this idea, to be asked for the recipe as so often happens. The Kashmiri masala when mixed with a tin of puréed tomatoes makes a quick and substantial curry and I like to throw in black-eyed beans and sweet potatoes and then warn everyone as this is not one of my milder curries. Many other curries combine nuts and vegetables (and, indeed, in New Zealand I have matched the macadamia nut with the local sweet potato, the kumara, to make a delightful curry) and in this chapter you will find the great combinations of peanuts with cauliflower and carrots with cashews. The common factor is that the cooking of the nuts in these curries softens them over time yet the texture is still a pleasing contrast in a range of curries where crunch is often missing. The Spinach and Lentil combination works really well, too, and I like the additional idea of throwing in some cubes of panir (Indian cheese).

I make a big thing of pickles at my demonstrations as there is no 'firepower' in the curries I cook there. Compensation for the mildness of my curries comes in the form of a wide ranging pickle table from the mildest of raitas with yogurt and cucumber or yogurt and coconut through to the hottest of chilli pickles and the hot and sour lime pickle. Some of these are best bought in Indian shops where they are both consistent and good value for money when bought in large tubs, but it is also a point of conversation to have a good range of home-made ones. The two most successful that I have made are aubergine (or brinjal) and grated raw green mango which can be hot if more chillis are used but, overall the effect is a refreshing tart chutney.

The patra leaves are a gorgeously soft and unusual dish, in the style of stuffed vineleaves and, obviously, variations on the stuffing ingredients will enable you to cook a range of such dishes. For instance, try using a lentil curry to stuff the patra leaves.

For this dinner party I felt I had to suggest a more unusual rice accompaniment, and the jackfruit is a wonderful ingredient as long as you do not have to peel and cut it yourself, as it is very sticky. The Biryani is the king of rice dishes and it is very convenient to cook in the oven which will be on anyway to keep the curries warm.

I have not included a dessert here as the Mango Fool and Srikand of *Vegetarian Dinner Parties* are difficult to beat but I have successfully used Sue's Boozy Bread and Butter Pudding from page 149 to finish off this meal.

One of the few ideal wines to accompany a curry meal – David Traeger Verdelho

Beer and Onion Bhajis

1 large onion, sliced into thin wedges	salt
	chilli powder to taste
150 g. gram flour	1 tsp. baking powder
1 tsp. cumin powder	200 ml. good real ale
1 tsp. coriander powder	oil for frying

1 Mix the gram flour with the spices, salt and baking powder.

2 Mix in sufficient ale to make a thick batter.

3 Just before frying the bhajis, mix in the onions so they are well coated in the batter.

4 Fry dessertspoonfuls of the onion and batter in hot oil for about 5 minutes until golden brown. Serve as soon as possible.

Samosas

2 tbsps. vegetable oil	1 carrot, cooked and chopped
1 small onion, finely chopped	2 tbsps. frozen peas
1 tsp. curry powder	salt
1 medium potato, cooked and chopped	filo pastry
	oil for frying

1 Fry the onion briefly in the oil and add the curry powder. Stir and continue to fry for a few minutes.

2 Stir in the vegetables and mix well.

3 Cut each piece of filo into two lengthways and place a good teaspoonful of the filling at the bottom of the strip of filo. Fold up making triangles as you go. These may be stored in the freezer until required and then fried from frozen.

4 Place the samosa into hot oil and fry quickly until brown.

Peanut and Cauliflower Curry

50 ml. vegetable oil
1 large onion, finely chopped
3 cloves garlic, finely chopped
2 cm. long piece ginger, grated or finely chopped
1 tsp. ground cumin
1 tsp. ground coriander

1 tsp. turmeric
half tsp. chilli powder
250 g. peanuts
400 g. tin tomatoes
300 g. cauliflower florets
salt

1 Fry the onion, garlic and ginger in the oil until transparent.

2 Add the spices and continue to fry for a few minutes.

3 Add in the peanuts and the tomatoes. Pour in sufficient water to cover the peanuts. Soaking the peanuts overnight prior to making this dish is a good idea.

4 Cook for about 30 minutes and add in the cauliflower and salt.

5 Continue to cook for a further 30 minutes or so and keep hot in a warm oven until required.

N.B. A Scottish friend taught me the trick of keeping your ginger in the freezer and grating it from frozen as and when required. This works well for horseradish, too.

Chinese Vegetable Curry

2 tbsps. Chinese Curry Sauce Concentrate
1 tin coconut cream
small tin sliced bamboo shoots
small tin water chestnuts, sliced
200 g. beansprouts

small tin straw mushrooms
300 g. broccoli florets, cooked
200 g. carrots, cooked (frozen are good here)
100 g. whole cashews

1 Mix all of the ingredients together and warm through.

Carrot and Cashew Curry

50 ml. vegetable oil
1 medium onion, finely chopped
2 cloves garlic, finely chopped
1 tsp. ground cumin
1 tsp. ground coriander
1 tsp. turmeric

500 g. carrots, peeled and chopped
250 g. cashew pieces
water (or use 500 ml. yogurt)
salt
2 tsps. garam masala
1 tbsp. coriander leaves, chopped

1 Fry the onion and garlic in the oil until transparent.

2 Stir in the spices and continue to fry for a few minutes.

3 Add the carrots (parboiling them would save time) and cashews and enough water to cover (or use yogurt).

4 Cook for up to 30 minutes until the carrots are tender and add in salt to taste and the garam masala and coriander leaves.

Spicy Kashmiri Sweet Potato Curry

2 tbsps. vegetable oil
1-2 tbsps. Kashmiri masala
400 g. tin tomatoes, puréed

500 g. sweet potatoes, cubed and parboiled
200 g. black-eyed beans, cooked

1 Mix the oil, Kashmiri masala and tomatoes and warm through.

2 Stir in the sweet potatoes and beans and continue to warm for a short while.

3 As with the other curries, when ready you can keep this warm in a low oven.

Spinach and Lentil Curry

250 g. green lentils (or toor dhal),
soaked overnight

1 tsp. turmeric

1 tsp. paprika

salt

1 large onion, finely chopped

50 ml. vegetable oil

800 g. tin spinach purée

2 tsps. black mustard seeds

1 tsp. cumin seeds

2 tbsps. lemon juice

2 tsps. garam masala

1 Cook the lentils on a low heat with the turmeric, paprika and salt until they are soft.

2 Fry the onion in the oil until transparent and add the whole spices. Continue to fry for a few minutes.

3 Add in the lentils and spinach, stir well and warm through.

4 Finally add the garam masala and lemon juice and keep warm in a low oven.

Stuffed Patra Leaves

1 packet patra leaves

500 g. mashed potato

2 tbsps. oil

2 tsps. black mustard seeds

4 cloves garlic, finely chopped

4 tbsps. coriander leaves

salt

2 tbsps. lemon juice

water

1 Fry the garlic and mustard seeds in the oil and stir into the mashed potato with the coriander leaves and salt. If you like, add in some finely chopped chillis.

2 On a flattened out patra leaf, place a good tablespoonful of the filling at the base of the leaf. Fold up the bottom of the leaf, fold in the edges and roll up to make a neat package.

3 Place in an oven-proof dish, pour over the lemon juice and enough water to come halfway up the patra leaf cylinders.

4 Cover the dish with a lid or with foil and cook in a moderate oven at 180°C, 350°F, gas mark 4 for 40 minutes, basting occasionally. Alternatively, and better, clingfilm and microwave for 15 minutes.

Serve with the spinach and lentil curry or with
the tomato soup (see page 81) as a sauce.

137

Aubergine Pickle

350 ml. vegetable oil
1 tsp. fenugreek
1 tsp. cumin seeds
1 tsp. mustard seeds
1 tbsp. puréed garlic
1 tbsp. puréed ginger
250 ml. red wine vinegar
2 tsps. chilli powder

1 tsp. turmeric
1 kg. aubergines, cut into small cubes
2 tbsps. sugar
salt
6 green chillis, slit from top to bottom

1 Heat the oil and fry the fenugreek, mustard seeds and cumin along with the ginger and garlic.

2 After a few minutes add in the vinegar, chilli powder and turmeric.

3 Add the remaining ingredients and simmer for as long as it takes to soften the aubergines.

4 Cool and store in the refrigerator or freezer.

Raw Green Mango Chutney

500 g. green mangoes
salt
1 tsp. turmeric
2 tsps. mustard powder
50 ml. vegetable oil

6 green chillis
3 cloves garlic, crushed
1 tbsp. black mustard seeds
250 ml. red wine vinegar

1 Peel and grate the mangoes. Stir in the salt, turmeric and mustard powder.

2 Fry the chillis, garlic and, after a couple of minutes, the mustard seeds. When the mustard seeds stop spluttering, add the vinegar and pour this mixture over the mangoes.

3 Mix and serve or refrigerate for up to 3 weeks.

Jackfruit Biryani

250 g. white basmati rice
2 cardamoms
1 piece cinnamon
15-20 strands saffron
salt
60 ml. vegetable oil
2 green chillis
1 tsp. ground cumin
half tsp. turmeric

1 tsp. ground coriander
2 cloves garlic, finely chopped
1 tsp. finely chopped fresh ginger
about 400 g. jackfruit (tinned green jackfruit, not in sugar syrup, is fine)
250 ml. sour cream
40 g. blanched almonds, lightly toasted

1 Boil the rice for 5 minutes with the cardamoms, cinnamon, saffron and salt. Drain well.

2 Place the oil, jackfruit, spices, sour cream and rice in an oven proof dish and cover. Bake in a moderate oven at 180°C, 350°F, gas mark 4 for an hour or so and serve garnished with the almonds. You may like to add some cooked lentils to the biryani and to garnish further with some hard-boiled eggs.

Chapter Twelve

Guest Recipes

🥄 have a large number of friends who enjoy gourmet vegetarian food and I am very happy that some of them have contributed ideas for this chapter. Many others, too numerous to mention, have helped with my research over the years and I take this opportunity to thank them.

Ron & Pam

Andrew

Andreas with "friend"

Sue & Fran

Steve

Marianne & Peter

Tina

Loredana

Andreas's Marinated Vegetables and Beans

Andreas Michli has a very interesting Cypriot food shop in St Ann's Road, Tottenham and many hundreds of recipe ideas that he is happy to pass on when you are in his shop. He cures many different types of olives and preserves a lot of vegetables which are for sale there and I give thanks to him for the recipes below as well as for the Greek Vegetable Stew in chapter ten.

FOR THE CAULIFLOWER:
1 large cauliflower
3 tbsps. lemon juice
salt
FOR THE MARINADE:
75 ml. lemon juice
60 ml. white wine vinegar

250 ml. extra virgin olive oil
2 tbsps. black mustard seeds, crushed
1 tbsp. mustard powder
6 cloves garlic, crushed
salt

1 Cut the cauliflower into spears and plunge into boiling water with lemon juice and salt. Once the water has returned to the boil leave for just 3 minutes.

2 Plunge the cauliflower into cold water immediately. Place the cauliflower, closely packed, into a deep dish.

3 Blend well all the other ingredients and pour over the cauliflower to cover.

4 Leave for 3 days at room temperature before serving.

FOR THE AUBERGINES:
2 medium aubergines, sliced and salted for an hour

3 tbsps. olive oil
FOR THE MARINADE:
100 ml. lemon juice
75 ml. red wine vinegar

300 ml. olive oil
2 tbsps. mint, chopped
2 tbsps. dill leaves, chopped
2 tbsps. coriander leaves, chopped
1 medium onion, thinly sliced
6 cloves garlic, very thinly sliced
salt

1 Drain the aubergines and dry. Brush with some olive oil and bake until just soft.

2 Place the aubergine slices in a dish and mix the other ingredients together. Pour the marinade over the aubergines to cover.

3 Leave for 3 days at room temperature before serving.

FOR THE BROAD BEANS:
300 g. dried broad beans, with the black end cut off
water
FOR THE MARINADE:
200 ml. extra virgin olive oil
salt

8 cloves garlic, finely chopped
6 tbsps. parsley or coriander, finely chopped
12 small tomatoes, finely chopped
2 tsps. ground cumin
200 ml. red wine vinegar

1 Soak the beans overnight and cook for about 30 minutes until they are soft.

2 Place the beans in a bowl and mix in the herbs, salt, garlic and cumin. Stir in also the tomatoes and pour over the vinegar and olive oil while the beans are still hot.

3 Store for 1-3 days at room temperature before serving.

Ron's Laver Bread Mousse

I have known Ron and Pam since 1973 and they have been good to me in so many ways. They run a lovely hotel, "The Windsor Lodge" in the centre of Swansea and I have spent many a merry Christmas there, several summer holiday breaks enjoying the beauty of the Gower beaches and the delights of picnics overlooking a waterfall several kilometres from the roadside near Glynneath. I have worked there (indeed, all the photography for *Vegetarian Dinner Parties* was done there) and relaxed there and I have been inspired there by Ron and Pam's gift of producing some great dishes and perfectly cooked vegetables. Swansea Market, just five minutes walk from the hotel, is full of very fresh vegetables and the strange ingredient, laver bread, a seaweed. It is bought in small packets, with or without oatmeal and it is often eaten for breakfast with a traditional fried selection. This recipe is Ron's successful attempt to upgrade this ingredient by turning it into a highly presentable and tasty starter. Ron's latest idea is to use a laver bread and cream mixture to top a moussaka; his version uses Welsh lamb!

450 g. laver bread
rind and juice of 2 lemons
4 eggs, separated
dozen or so basil leaves, chopped

150 ml. crème fraîche
good pinch freshly ground black pepper

1 Mix the laver bread with the lemon rind and juice, the egg yolks, basil leaves, cream and pepper.

2 Whisk the egg whites until light and fold them into the laver bread mixture.

3 Pour the mixture into a soufflé dish and place this dish in another with a couple of centimetres of water.

4 Cook, bain-marie style, in a moderate oven at 180°C, 350°F, gas mark 4 for 30 minutes covered.

Andrew's Siny'et Bedingal

Andrew is a gourmet vegan and he has maintained a reputation since I have known him for interesting dinner parties by constantly expanding his repertoire through travel and a love of trying out new ideas. This recipe works and does not have the greasiness of some non-vegan aubergine layer dishes.

2 large aubergines
sunflower oil for frying
8 cloves garlic, crushed
2 tbsps. tomato purée
salt
1 tbsp. apple juice concentrate
half tsp. ground cumin

half tsp. paprika
half tsp. black pepper
juice of 1 lemon
1 tbsp. vinegar
TO GARNISH:
coriander leaves

1 Slice the aubergines 1 centimetre thick and salt. Leave for 1 hour and squeeze firmly.

2 Fry the slices in the oil until soft and drain.

3 Blend the garlic, tomato purée, salt, apple juice concentrate and seasonings and add sufficient water to mix to a loose paste.

4 Layer the aubergines with this sauce and pour over a further 75 ml. of water.

5 Cover and cook slowly for 10 minutes.

6 Allow to cool and place in the refrigerator for 6 hours. Serve hot or cold garnished with coriander leaves. Eat with Turkish bread (or Steve's bread, see page 150).

Andreas's Moussaka

150 ml. olive oil

500 g. Cyprus potatoes, in half cm. slices

1 medium aubergine, sliced lengthways

2 courgettes, sliced lengthways

100 g. parmesan or pecorino, grated

FOR THE TOMATO SAUCE:

2 tbsps. olive oil

4 spring onions, chopped

4 cloves garlic, finely chopped

400 g. tin tomatoes, puréed

1 tsp. dried oregano

1 tsp. dried basil

2 tbsps. fresh mint

2 tbsps. flour

white wine if necessary

FOR THE BECHAMEL SAUCE:

50 g. butter

2 tbsps. flour

500 ml. milk

1-2 bayleaves

salt

good pinch black pepper

pinch nutmeg

80 g. Gruyère cheese, grated

1 Fry the vegetables separately in the olive oil until they are just tender.

2 Make the tomato sauce: fry the onion and garlic in the olive oil until transparent. Stir in the tomatoes and herbs and cook for a few minutes. Add in the flour and cook for several minutes adding the white wine if necessary to make a thick sauce.

3 Make the bechamel sauce: melt the butter and stir in the flour for a minute or so. Slowly add the milk, stirring constantly. Throw in the bayleaves and season. Cook for about 7 minutes and stir in the cheese. Stir well until the cheese is melted.

4 Assemble the moussaka: put a layer of potatoes at the bottom of an ovenproof dish so that the bottom is completely covered. Pour in a half centimetre layer of the tomato sauce and a sprinkle of the grated parmesan. Continue with a layer of aubergines, another layer of tomato sauce and parmesan and finish with a layer of courgettes. Pour over the bechamel sauce and bake in the middle of a moderate oven at 180°C, 350°F, gas mark 4 for an hour until brown on top. If the moussaka browns too soon, cover it with some foil.

Other vegetables such as peppers, pumpkin or leeks may be used in the layers and a similar dish may be done with cabbage and rice where the rice is cooked in a fair amount of liquid as the dish is in the oven.

Loredana's Suppli

I am not inclined to be a landlord but when I came into a flat in Goodmayes in 1997, it proved easier to let than to sell. I was fortunate that my tenant brought me many ideas from her native Rome (as well as gifts of parmesan and fine Italian wine). Additionally, she has often worked well for me at my cookery demonstrations.

500 g. organic short-grain brown rice

60 ml. olive oil

1 medium onion, finely chopped

2 cloves garlic, finely chopped

1 medium carrot, chopped

2 sticks celery, chopped

50 g. basil, chopped (or 1 tsp. dried)

50 g. parsley, finely chopped

salt

generous pinch black pepper

400 g. tin tomatoes

stock and/or white wine

50 g. grated parmesan

3 eggs, beaten

breadcrumbs

200 g. mozzarella

olive oil for frying

1 To make the sauce, fry the onion and garlic briefly in the oil and throw in the carrots and celery. After a couple of minutes add the herbs and season well.

2 Add the tomatoes to the sauce and stir in the rice. Cover with stock and/ or white wine and add more from time to time so that the rice is always covered. After 45 minutes the rice should be soft.

3 Stir the parmesan into the rice and add the eggs. Allow to cool and refrigerate for a while.

4 Form the suppli into small rugger ball shapes by shaping some rice around a small cube of mozzarella. Roll it in breadcrumbs and, when they have all been shaped, fry in hot olive oil until golden brown all over.

This recipe makes over twenty suppli, but Loredana insists that it is a recipe for 6 because everyone eats a lot of rice in Rome. Although they are, undoubtedly, delicious, if you were to serve them with a selection of other dishes, my feeling is that one is sufficient and so you may want to divide the recipe by 3 or so.

Tina's White Chocolate Cheesecake
(to die for)

Tina began work at The Windsor Lodge Hotel several years ago as a kitchen hand. Over time her talents have become clear and now she has taken over much of the preparation and serving of the starters and desserts. This recipe should make her famous.

FOR THE BASE:
1 pkt. Amaretti biscuits
100 g. unsalted butter, melted
FOR THE MIDDLE LAYER:
400 g. white chocolate
1 kg. fromage frais
2 tsps. agar (optional)

FOR THE TOPPING:
100 ml. crème de cassis
120 g. blueberries

1 Blend the amaretti biscuits with the melted butter (or use some liqueur and, maybe, some ground almonds as in the Tira Mi Su, see page 85). Press this mixture well into the base of a 25 cm. flan dish.

2 Melt the white chocolate and stir in the fromage frais and the agar, if used. Pour this mixture over the base and put in a refrigerator for a few hours or overnight.

3 Warm the cassis and cook the blueberries gently for 4 or 5 minutes in it.

4 Serve slices of the cheesecake with spoonfuls of the blueberries poured over each slice.

A mixture of framboise and raspberries or fraise and strawberries would be just as good.

Sue's Boozy Bread and Butter Pudding

This recipe will appear in Susan Nowak's first cookery book, on cooking with beer, likely to be called "Hop Cuisine", to be published early in 1999 by Faber & Faber. She is also the Editor of the Campaign for Real Ale guidebook "Good Pub Food", fifth edition to be published in Spring 1999, a columnist in "What's Brewing" and regular broadcaster/writer in the national media on pub food, cooking with beer and beer to drink with food. She has also won both the Silver and Pewter Tankard in the Beer Writer of the Year awards. In addition, Sue and her husband have been good friends for many years and we have shared many a dinner party and mushroom hunt. She has been very supportive of all my ventures and writes most eloquently on many matters.

100 g. raisins	**demerara sugar**
50 g. chopped dates	**450 ml. milk**
300 ml. barley wine	**2 eggs, whisked**
butter to grease the dish	**pinch nutmeg**
6 thin slices brown bread, buttered	**1 tsp. ground cinnamon**
and with the crusts removed	

1 Place the raisins and dates in a bowl and pour over the barley wine. Leave for up to 48 hours until the fruit is swollen with the liquor then drain, retaining any unabsorbed beer.

2 Butter an oblong ovenproof dish, cut the bread into triangles and layer it in the dish, butter side up, sprinkling each layer with the soaked fruit and sugar to taste, finishing with bread.

3 Warm the milk without boiling and pour it over the eggs, whisking it in. Pour this over the bread until it is almost covered and leave to stand for 20 minutes.

4 Pour some of the retained beer over the bread and finish with a grating of nutmeg and the powdered cinnamon.

5 Bake in a preheated oven at 190°C, 375°F, gas mark 5 above the centre of the oven for 30-35 minutes until crisp on top, melting underneath and risen to almost souffle lightness. (You do not need a whole half pint of beer, but barley wine flavoured by the fruit is a luscious cook's perk or it can be used to flavour custard).

Steve's Feta Cheese, Potato and Thyme Bread

Steve's mother, Sue has been helping me since 1986 and her help and support has been invaluable in keeping my operation smooth at many a festival. Steve came along to assist at WOMAD in 1996 at the age of 18 with no real direction in life. His mother was unsure how well he would fit in. By the end of the festival he was a changed person. He had spent many hours producing many bucketfuls of mayonnaise and over 50 large spinach pies a day. He did this job with great skill and energy in warm conditions and enjoyed the experience so much he soon started a job in catering and has been very successful and creative. Now he has the ambition to open his own restaurant.

110 g. feta cheese, cubed	**1 tsp. thyme, chopped**
5 spring onions, finely sliced	**1 egg**
175 g. red potatoes	**2 tbsps. milk**
175 g. self-raising wholemeal flour	**1 tsp. whole-grain mustard**
salt	**flour for dusting**
pinch cayenne pepper	

1 Peel and coarsely grate the potato.

2 Add in the flour, salt and cayenne. Add the spring onions, thyme and 70 g. of the cheese. Blend well.

3 Beat the egg with the milk and mustard then blend in with the flour and potato mixture to make a loose, rough dough.

4 Transfer it to a baking sheet which has been well greased and pat gently to make a 15 cm. diameter round, flat loaf. Lightly press the remainder of the cheese over the surface and dust with flour.

5 Bake in the middle of a moderate oven at 190°C, 375°F, gas mark 5 for 40-45 minutes until golden brown.

6 Transfer to a cooling tray and serve when still slightly warm.

Marianne and Peter's
Rich Chocolate Cake (Gluten Free)

Marianne and Peter are two wonderful like-minded people who have helped me at festivals with great skill and flair. They work at Community Wholefoods providing tasty lunches for the workers there. Additionally, they do outside catering and often demonstrate their skills at food shows.

150 g. good quality chocolate (min. 65% cocoa solids)

150 g. unsalted butter

160 g. demerara sugar

4 med. eggs, separated

40 g. cocoa powder

150 g. ground almonds

1 tsp. baking powder

1 Set the oven to 180°C, 350°F, gas mark 4. Grease and line a 20 cm. springform tin.

2 Place the butter and chocolate in a bowl over lightly simmering water until melted, stirring occasionally.

3 Beat together the egg yolks and sugar and add the melted butter and chocolate. Next add the cocoa powder, ground almonds and baking powder and mix well.

4 In a separate bowl, whisk the egg whites until stiff and fold into the chocolate mixture.

5 Pour the mixture into the prepared tin and level the surface. Bake for 35-40 minutes until firm to the touch. Leave to cool in the tin for approximately 30 minutes and then turn it out. It may be served as a dessert with crème fraîche or whipped cream.

Leon with Bob McLean
of the great St. Hallett
winery at 'The Great
Australian Wine Tasting'
in London.
His neighbours in the
Barossa Valley have
nicknamed him
"Sir Lunchalot".

Leon with David Traeger,
maker of the best Verdelho
and Bill Sneddon of the
excellent Allandale winery
in the Hunter Valley

The LEN EVANS Theory of Capacity (see page 12)

THERE IS AN AWFUL LOT OF WINE IN THE WORLD, but there is also a lot of awful wine.

NO SENSIBLE PERSON DRINKS TO EXCESS, therefore any one person can only drink a certain amount in a lifetime.

THERE ARE COUNTLESS FLAVOURS, nuances, shades of wine; endless varieties, regions, styles. You have neither the time nor the capacity to try them all.

TO MAKE THE MOST OF THE TIME LEFT TO YOU, you must start by calculating your total future capacity. One bottle a day is 365 bottles a year. If your life expectancy is another 30 years, there are only 10,000 odd bottles ahead of you.

PEOPLE WHO SAY: *"YOU CAN'T DRINK THE GOOD STUFF ALL THE TIME"* ARE TALKING RUBBISH. You <u>must</u> drink good stuff all the time. Every time you drink a bottle of inferior wine, it's like smashing a superior bottle against the wall. The pleasure is lost forever – you can't get that bottle back.

THERE ARE PEOPLE WHO BUILD UP HUGE CELLARS, most of which they have no hope of drinking. They are foolish in over-estimating their capacity, but they err on the right side *and their friends love them.*

THERE ARE ALSO PEOPLE WHO DON'T WANT TO DRINK GOOD WINE, and are happy with the cheapies. I forgive them. There are others who are content with beer and spirits; I can't worry about everybody.

WINE IS NOT MEANT TO BE ENJOYED FOR ITS OWN SAKE. It is the key to love and laughter with friends, to the enjoyment of food, beauty and humour and art and music. Its rewards are far beyond its cost.

WHAT PART IS WINE OF YOUR LIFE? Ten percentum: Ergo, 10 per cent of your income should be spent on wine.

THE PRINCIPLE SHOULD BE APPLIED TO OTHER PHASES OF LIFE. A disciple kissed a beautiful young lady and she demurred. He was aghast, and said: "Don't get the wrong idea. I've worked out I can only make love another 1343 times. I'm bloody sure I'm not wasting one on you!"

A brief guide for wine lovers

Menu and choice of wines No hard and fast rules, but errors are avoided and your guests will be satisfied when: a) White wine precedes red wine; b) A young wine precedes an older wine; c) A light wine precedes a fuller bodied wine.

Complementing wine and food A balance is easily found with the common sense rule: Light dishes are suited by a light wine; Country/provincial dishes are suited by a young, vigorous wine; Haute Cuisine is suited by top rank wines.

Dry white wines and the lighter reds suit lighter dishes and mild flavoured cheeses; rosé wines can be served throughout light meals; the finest red wines superbly accompany a well chosen and varied cheese board.

Glasses Choose light, stemmed glasses sufficiently large to leave room for the bouquet to develop. Tulip shaped for white, rosé and sparkling. Balloon shaped for red wines. Avoid perfumed detergents, always rinse in fresh water, dry with a clean cloth and store in cupboards free from odours of paint or varnish.

Serving wines

Temperature:

Sparkling wines	40°F (6 - 8°C)	Young reds and whites	50°F (10 - 12°C)
Fine white wines	50°F (12 - 14°C)	Fine red wines	60°F (16 - 17°C)

Cooling:
Two hours in the refrigerator door or half an hour in an ice bucket is ample.

Warming:
Heat is wine's worst enemy. Never suddenly warm wine from too cold. Allow the bottle to warm up progressively at room temperature

Pulling the cork out:
Cut the capsule well below the top, wipe the neck clean and gently draw the cork with a corkscrew long enough to pierce totally the cork. Taste the wine.

Decanting:
Most wines do not require this and can be served direct from the bottle. Use a cradle basket for wine that has acquired a deposit.

Pouring out:
Never fill glasses full. Leave plenty of room for the bouquet to blossom up in the glass.

The LEON LEWIS Theory of Vegetarianism

There are many signs of a trend towards vegetarianism. The fact that we are now consuming less meat per head than during the Depression of the 30's is because of the overwhelming case for a vegetarian diet, summarised below.

Better health A balanced vegetarian diet supplies everything that the human body requires. Moreover, vegetarian suffer less from some cancers (colon and breast) and from heart disease, than the population as a whole. Additionally, the production of meat involves the overuse of antibiotics to control disease in livestock.

Ecology A vegetarian diet would mean more food for all as it takes 10 units by weight of animal feed to produce 1 unit of meat. Gandhi said: "It is wonderful, if we chose the right diet, what an extraordinarily small quantity would suffice." The waste products of meat production cause pollution and the destruction of the rainforests in the quest for cheaper meat has led to a speeding up of the greenhouse effect.

Cost On average it is cheaper to live on a vegetarian diet (notwithstanding some of the ingredients used in this book!)

History Throughout history many great philosophers and thinkers have recommended vegetarianism: Pythagoras, Socrates, Newton, Einstein, Shelley and Wagner to name a few.

Bible In Genesis it is written: "And God said: behold I have given you every herb-bearing seed upon the earth, and all trees that have in themselves seed of their own kind, to be your meat." In the original version of the Bible, written in Greek, the word for meat occurred nowhere at all.

Biological Evidence John Wynne-Tyson has pointed out that we are naturally herbivorous. He points out that we do not have claws, we have longish bowels that deal well with fruits and grains, we sweat to control our body heat rather than panting, and we suck to imbibe fluids rather than lapping as do carnivorous animals.

And Finally My view is that after a period of adjustment and re-education of your cooking habits and taste buds you will find that vegetarian food not only does you good, but it tastes good. It was George Bernard Shaw who said "There is no love sincerer than the love of food."